50th ANNIVERSARY EDITION
BY THIS SHALL WE BE KNOWN

50th ANNIVERSARY EDITION
BY THIS SHALL WE BE KNOWN

Interpreting the Voice,
Vision and Message of
Martin Luther King Jr.

TERRIEL R. BYRD

READERSMAGNET, LLC

Dedicated to Geneva Byrd,
my mother she prayed for me!

CONTENTS

PROLOGUE

---------- ❋ ----------

The declining role of the modern Civil Rights Movement: 21st Century Challenge

OVER THE PAST SEVERAL decades, the Civil Rights Movement of the fifties and sixties has nearly lost its national significance. Sadly, for the first time in decades, young people have little recollection of the role played by organizations such as SCLC (Southern Christian Leadership Conference), CORE (Congress of Racial Equality), and PUSH (People United to Save America). Even the NAACP (National Association for the Advancement of Colored People and NUL (National Urban League) remain just slightly more active than many of the other previously mentioned groups, their relevance to many, and mostly people of color, even remains questionable. Today, the "Black Lives Matters" movement has taken up the mantle of protest. The "Mee too" movement, founded by Tarana Burke, created to help young women of color who survived sexual abuse and assault, has now inspired solidarity, amplifies the voices of thousands of victims of sexual abuse, and puts the focus back on survivors.[1]

---

[1] Tarana Burke, https://www.kepplerspeakers.com/speakers/tarana-burke (2017 speakers)

The challenges today are as stark and compelling as were the challenges of the 50s and 60s, yet the coordinated efforts of civil rights groups, to confront the challenges is mostly nonexistent. I suggest that there are at least three distinct causes for the decline of the modern Civil Rights Movement. Each of the reasons collectively has contributed to a weakening of the effectiveness of the movement. This book will examine Dr. King's vision, voice and messages as well as propose ways in which the Civil Rights Movement of the fifties and sixties can reclaim its viability and relevance once again.

By far the most significant factor related to the decline of the Civil Rights Movement was the 1968 assassination of its inspirational icon, the civil rights movements' most prolific leader, Dr. Martin Luther King, Jr. Without a doubt, Dr. King was everything the movement stood for and everything the movement hoped and aspired for. In that one dreadful episode, King's death stifled his dream, his vision and his voice, those ideals which were the embodiment of vigor and aspirations of hope for millions around the world. April 4, 1968 is now forever etched in the consciousness of justice loving people, as the day the dream was transformed into a nightmare.

The second factor contributing to the demise of the modern civil rights movement could be viewed as an ideological shift. It was certainly apparent that the early civil rights movement found its home in the black church. Not only was the black church a refuge from a hostile racist society; the black church was also considered a base of operation for the activities of the movement. Followers of the movement were informed regarding the direction, the plans shared with them from the movements' leaders. Inspirational and motivational speeches were given. The black church also brought with it a clearly defined theological framework, a. The "Black Lives Matters movement" is one example of the visible absence of the collective church as a core institution backing the movement. During the seventies and eighties, the moral mandate based largely on faith, family, and, more importantly, the Holy Scriptures, which was showing signs of decay, a shift away from the traditional values of the black church, and greater emphasis was placed on political expediency. Primarily, under the black leadership of Jesse Jackson, Al Sharpton and other progressives, the attempt was to unite behind other groups who shared similar political interest. The LBGT (lesbian, gay, bisexual, and transgender) also found a home by yoking themselves to the wagon of the civil movements. In doing so, this gave a level of credibility and visibility to these groups. While these other groups enlarged the tent, the Civil Rights movement became severely polarized. For example, The Reverend Fred Shuttlesworth, longtime civil rights leader, was quoted as saying "...I personally strongly oppose same sex marriages," and he continued with, "I recognize that the SCLC is not just a civil rights organization, or human rights organization. We are also a church-based Organization! And in church, we are taught to pray for all God's children!"[2] While most evangelical churches (black and white) held fast to traditional teaching on Homosexuality as sinful and immoral, gay rights, as important as it might be relative to human rights, rarely was viewed by the black church as a civil rights issue on par with racial injustice. Older stewards of the modern civil rights era became less interested in supporting rallies that no longer had racial injustice as its primary focus.

By the end of the Obama administration and the start of the Trump administration, the social climate in America had changed drastically. June 17, 2015, nine people were shot and killed during a Bible study session at Emanuel African Methodist Episcopal Church in Charleston, South Carolina. The shooter Dylann Roof, a 21 year old young man, committed an act of domestic terrorism spawned on by racial hatred. Jul 9, 2016, in Dallas Texas, during a "Black Lives Matter" rally, a 25 year old African American, Micah Xavier Johnson, in a "military style sniper attack" practiced his hateful brand of vigilante justice, killing 5 police officers. In some ways, old racial wounds of the past were opened leaving a clear window into

---

2   Nathaniel Livingston "SCLC's Rev. Fred Shuttlesworth Opposes Same Sex Marriages" http://blackcincinnati.blogspot.com/2004/08/sclcs-rev-fred-shuttlesworth-opposes.html (7 August, 2004)

resemblance of the past. In many ways, Ferguson became the new Birmingham, and Maryland the new Chicago. After all, Ferguson Missouri had a long history of racial tension. Things came to a head in Ferguson when Michael Brown, an unarmed black teenager, was shot and killed on Aug. 9, 2014 by Darren Wilson, a white police officer in Ferguson, Mo., a suburb of St. Louis. The shooting prompted protests that roiled the area for weeks. On Nov. 24, the St. Louis County prosecutor announced that a grand jury decided not to indict Mr. Wilson. The announcement set off another wave of protests. In March, the Justice Department called on Ferguson to overhaul its criminal justice system, declaring that the city had engaged in constitutional violations. [3] Nationwide outrage was felt on both sides, not unlike Birmingham, with its racially divided population. Many of the white citizens were not immediately impressed by the national attention given to their gentile society. After all, the social construct was well defined, meaning the status quo society where everyone (black and white) knew his or her place. In 1963, Dr. Martin Luther King, Jr. provided a clear description of what it would be like to be black living in Birmingham, Ala:

> You would be born in a jim-crow hospital to parents who probably lived in the ghetto. You would attend a jim-crow school. It is not really true that the city fathers had never heard of the Supreme Court's school-desegregation order. They had heard of it and, since its passage, had consistently expressed their defiance, typified by the prediction of one official that blood would run in the streets before desegregation would be permitted to come to Birmingham. [4]

---

[3]   The New York Times "http:What Happened in Ferguson" //www. nytimes.com/interactive/2014/08/13/us/ferguson-missouri-town-under-siege-after-police-shooting.html?_r=0Q&A UPDATED Aug. 10, 2015

[4]   Martin Luther King, Jr. *Why We Can't Wait* (New York, Signet Books, 1964), 47—48.

The white establishment in St. Louis was profoundly aware of history, and did not want their city to be seen as another Birmingham, Alabama. They "silenced" civil rights agitation by working with the black elite to maintain a public show of social of harmony.

"The unrest in Ferguson in August 2014 is rooted in Missouri's particularly acute levels of racial segregation. Missouri's African-American population is heavily concentrated in the metropolitan areas of St. Louis and Kansas City, both of which are, in themselves, deeply segregated. Among the 100 largest cities in the United States, the city of St. Louis is the fifth-most racially segregated."[5]

The protest following the Freddy Grey death in Baltimore Maryland resembled the protest of the sixties in Chicago. What stood out in Chicago was, "not only did the Chicago Freedom Movement forever change the way the people of Chicago lived, it highlighted the tremendous problems that would confront the movement as it sought to bring the struggle to the big cities of the North."[6] Gray was a 25-year-old African-American who died while in police custody. Gray died after being taken into custody in an arrest involving three white and three African-American Baltimore police officers.

The officers have been charged with multiple offenses, including murder and manslaughter, and the Department of Justice has conducted a "pattern-and-practices" investigation of allegations of

---

[5] Daniel Marans, Mariah Stewart, Black Voices "Why Ferguson has become the heart of racial tension in America" https://www.huffingtonpost.com/entry/ferguson-mizzou-missouri-racial-tension_us_564736e2e4b08cda3488f34d (16 November 2015)

[6] Elliott C. Mclaughlin, Ben Brumfield and Dana Ford "Freddie Gray Death: Questions many, answers few, emotions high in Baltimore" http://www.cnn.com/2015/04/20/us/baltimore-freddie-gray-death/index.html (20 April 2015).

racial discrimination in the city's police department.[7] All charges were dropped against the police officers.

> These are tragic events along with the June 21, 2016 shooting of Philando Castile, who was shot by a Minnesota, police officer. The public outrage was sparked as a result of Castile's girlfriend's live streaming of the interaction between the police officer and Castile. As Castile attempted to explain to the officer that he was a legal gun owner and carried a concealed weapon, within seconds fatal shots were fired from the officers' revolver. He said ""I thought he had a gun in his hand," Yanez said later. Yanez feared for his life, he said, and the lives of his partner as well as the two passengers in the car: Castile's girlfriend and her young daughter. Recounting the shooting the following day, Yanez said: "I thought I was gonna die. And, I was scared because, I didn't know if he was gonna, I didn't know what he was gonna do." The police officer was acquitted in the killing of Philando Castile.[8] The Castile killing prompted protest in many cities. In the end, each of the tragic cases aforementioned revealed a deep longing for a calm, resolute voice of reason that could penetrate the anger and unbridled passion surrounding those involved. There is a thirst, a genuine thirst for the vision, voice and message of Martin Luther King, Jr., in this age. The words of Jesus, "Blessed are the peacemakers, for they will be called children of God" could not be more relevant to this 20th century prophet of peace.

---

[7] Elliott C. Mclaughlin, Ben Brumfield and Dana Ford "Freddie Gray Death: Questions many, answers few, emotions high in Baltimore" http://www.cnn.com/2015/04/20/us/baltimore-freddie-gray-death/index.html (20 April 2015).

[8] Mark Berman "What the police officer who shot Philando Castile said about the shooting"Pttps://www.washingtonpost.com/news/post-nation/wp/2017/06/21/what-the-police-officer-who-shot-philando-tcastile-said-about-the-shooting/?utm_term=.9d7dcfae1840 (21 July 2017).

America founding fathers pledged to each other, our lives, our fortunes and our sacred honor, in defense of liberty and freedom. Martin Luther king, Jr. was called upon to proclaim his vision for liberty and freedom in the land for all its inhabitants, and to extend the message of love and peace with justice and reconciliation to all nations. May the words found in this book foster and inspire each of us to reclaim Dr. King's Voice, Vision and Message for this century.

Martin Luther King's vision for social equality, his voice and message of justice and spiritual discernment give the fullest expression to the challenges now facing contemporary society in America and the world at large. The Civil Rights Movement of the twentieth century represented a world changing phenomenon unlike any before it on the stage of the human struggle for equality. It was that final push in a long line of movements for racial parity that yielded the open society long sought after for all people in America. It served as a model for the oppressed worldwide to capture a glimpse of hope out dungeons of despair. The enormity of this single accomplishment, though it had worldwide impact, however, should not overshadow the simple truths and practical wisdom that may still be gleaned from the preaching, the life and thought of Dr. Martin Luther King, Jr. Without question, his message is still relevant today as the world has crossed the bridge of the twenty first century and encounters more difficult continental and intercontinental human relations. As a result, the wisdom and passion couched in King's preaching and speeches are often sought out and repeated. His words are among the most widely quoted and reflected upon by scholars, activists and social thinkers from around the globe as the quest for peace and social freedom continues. Martin Luther Kings' vision still provides a foretaste into a future where the church can function as an effective agent of positive change that is able also to keep his ideas relevant. King longed to witness a church where there was dynamic transformation of the human spirit, where a more inclusive and vibrant worship takes place wielded together in the bond of peace as the beloved community. By this shall we be known!

CHAPTER ONE

King's Vision, Voice and Message for the 21st Century

———— ❋ ————

"I must preach the good news of the kingdom of God to the other towns as well; for I was sent for this purpose." Jesus of Nazareth (Luke 4:43)

ON MARCH 31, 1968, Dr. Martin Luther King, Jr. preached his last Sunday morning sermon at the national episcopal Cathedral at Washington, D.C. It revealed his thoughts on "Remaining awake through a Great Revolution." Obviously desiring to evoke a similar level of contemplation in his listeners, Dr. King, in this message, as he did with so many of his others, captivated his audience. Distinctive, creative and prophetic, King alluded to Rip Van Winkle, the n'er-do-well character who slept through a revolution, brought to life by Washington Irving, to illustrate the potential of one's losses when you simply dropped out of life.

> When Rip Van Winkle went up into the mountain, the sign had a picture of King George iii of England.

———

When he came down Twenty years later the sign had a picture of George Washington, the first president of the United States. When Rip Van Winkle looked up at the picture of George Washington, and looking at the picture he was amazed…he was completely lost—he knew not who he was. And this reveals to us that the most striking thing about the story of Rip Van Winkle is not merely that Rip slept twenty years, but that he slept through a revolution.[2]

Rip Van Winkle wanted to get away from the carping of his wife and the duties she often called upon him to perform. He didn't like responsibilities. This slothful man wanted nothing to do with the drudgeries of life. Even if it meant that his engagement in certain routines would produce positive changes for himself, his wife and his children. Instead, he chose to run for the hills. He dropped out of life for twenty years and slept through the noise and tumult of a revolution. Having decided to shut his eyes to his present realities, the revolution fundamentally changed his world as he knew it without his participation in it. Dr. King assumed a proactive stance in the sermon and appealed to the deepest and best of moral character in his addressees. He understood the smartness of Americans; that they were, innovative, creative and industrious. King, himself, also embodied these attributes. He wanted the best for the nation and used his vast intellect and immense moral persuasion to ensure that the living epistle, "all men are created equal", found its full expression in American life. If the nation was going to be indivisible, then it first had to be one nation. If, under God, it was going to achieve this status; then, it had to be healed of its near mortal divisions. He believed that his audience wanted this too. after all, the rest of the world watched and listened to what happened in America; and not only that—when Dr. King spoke of injustices committed against a human being in America, he spoke of injustices committed against human beings worldwide.

Grand change in an improbable situation was a clear revelation for Martin Luther King, Jr. King had seen improbability confronted and defeated when on May 17, 1954, Chief Justice earl Warren, read the United States supreme Court's unanimous decision of outlawing separate but equal public schools. Martin King lived history when he spearheaded the organized Montgomery Bus Boycott in 1955 that crippled the Montgomery, Alabama public transit system. However, life in America and in numerous pockets of the world remained improbable for those considered the under-classes. Africa and Asia were bristling cauldrons of racism, deprivation and colonization. He realized that change was inevitable: racial inequities, the war in Vietnam, rampant poverty for blacks and whites were unsustainable injustices he knew had to change, or the revolution was a date certain. Most important, he realized that change would happen when those who recognized that change was needed also acted.

In Dr. King's vision of that sermon—and it is hard to believe that nearly a half-century has passed since then—and, despite landmark Civil Rights legislation in 1964 and 1965 that opened life to blacks in America as it had never been opened before with voting rights, fair housing, and fair employment provisions—he saw the need for more transformation to come for the United States. He recognized that, even if there was no bloody revolution like the one through which Rip Van Winkle slept, a revolution nonetheless was destined to drastically change the national and global landscape. Those resistant to change and those comfortable with the status quo would sleep through it; those interested in nothing outside their own concerns would sleep through the revolution; those content with depriving and seeing others deprived of their rightful benefits as Americans would sleep through the revolution. As surely as Dr. King spoke of change to the audience seated at the Cathedral that day, he surely also spoke to every American who had an ear to hear the drumbeat for change, and to every politician who might have the courage to act more bravely and honorably than Rip Van Winkle. To convert America into the country that lived up to its exalted promises to all of its citizens and that lived up to its magnificent potentials as a good global citizen would require many people to tap into a new reservoir of valor, and spirituality.

Since Dr. King's final sermon, an enormous change has come to America, but not enough. Much of it would please him as his narrative of redemptive radical change continues to pierce the veil of time and significance. Yet, strongholds of poverty remain in every sector of the country; however, it was on the Louisiana Gulf Coast where the unforgiving power of Hurricane Katrina exposed such a scourge of poverty that it embarrassed the country. Human deprivations laid waste the lives of thousands of people, who had no-where to go and no-where to stay in a storm so terrible that it destroyed 1,800 lives and displaced hundreds of thousands more.

In Dr. King's day, the Vietnam War drained the United States treasury of billions of dollars, and killed or maimed soldiers and citizens. The loss of precious blood and resources launched King into a call for equality in the nation he so loved. Many found it objectionable that, he, a preacher, would speak to the issues of war. His detractors however, did not deter his belief that it was morally abhorrent to expend money on the war that could be used to bring parity of life to the poor; and it was equally abhorrent to him that poor white boys and poor black boys were forced to fight the war. Upon returning home, white boys and black boys were scorned for fighting the unpopular war. Poor black boys, for a time, would return home from Southeast Asia only to be treated as second-class citizens.

Because of King's concept of the Beloved Community, and if we had the privilege of hearing his opinion today, we would realize that he would have been distressed by America's adventuresome military activities in Iraq. Under the opaque circumstances which war was declared on Iraq and its people, no doubt he would have preferred ceaseless diplomacy rather than the chosen path of military violence. War as opposed to peace was a moral choice for King— peace for which he advocated as a disciple of and as a declaration of Christ, "Blessed are the peacemakers for they shall be called the children of God." King warned that hate is the only true victor in the aftermath of war, "We say that war is the consequence of hate, but close scrutiny reveals this sequence: First fear, then hate, then war, and finally deeper hatred."[3] Nobody can win in a war.

"The choice today is no longer between violence and nonviolence. It is either nonviolence or nonexistence,"[4] King's vision of the Beloved Community is achievable only when all humanity resolves to overcome fear through faith, when humankind will overcome oppression and violence without resorting to acts of senseless, inhumane violence and oppression.

Suffice it to say that his vision of transformational change has been partially encompassed by the revolution he foresaw. Hunger for transformation of American life led to the landslide election of Barack Obama as the forty-fourth President of the United States. Of selflessness and of spirituality, his message is relevant today. After forty years, a lingering vacuum for King's brand of leadership exists. It appeared to many that the previous administrations, both Democratic and Republican economic policies, favored the wealthy, and neglected the middle and lower class workers. Unemployment for blacks, according to the Center for American Progress, dropped 0.1 percent every year since 2000 after rising steadily since 1990.[5] Real median income for every American household declined in 2008 and the overall poverty rate, according to the United States Census Bureau rose to 13.2 percent as millions of American workers, who lost jobs, were forced into destitution and homelessness.

Dr. King's disquiet, which included social slumber, idleness, disengagement, and hostility that leads to war and death and lack of concern about the common welfare of humanity are still cankers eating away at the fabric of life in America and the world. It is still his disquiet. He recognized that if life in America could not work for all, it could not work for any. America still does not provide the sanctuary for all its citizens as Dr. King hoped for. Dr. King's message can be closely interpreted to mean that we are responsible to and for one another. The ongoing resonance of his voice, vision and message is that we should all pick up the blood stained banner and charge ahead to fight for human dignity and equality both here in America and elsewhere.

Today's leaders must follow in the framework of Dr. King's ethical dimensions. Like King, they should be sober, vigilant and exhibits the breadth and depth of personal counsel that supports an America government that embraces humaneness, authenticity of ideas and wholesomeness that leads to civic life that provides adequately for all in America. It is hoped that by the strength and character of these concepts, we shall be known.

Ebenezer Baptist Church—Martin's childhood church and the church he co-pastored with his father Daddy King

CHAPTER TWO

Sunday Morning:
Thy Kingdom Come,
Thy Will Be Done

---- ❋ ----

*"The Spirit of the Lord GOD is upon me, because the LORD
has anointed me to bring good news to the poor;" Isa. 61:1 ESV*

OVER THE SHORT YEARS of the ministry of Dr. Martin Luther
King, Jr., we see him change and become more urgent about
matters of social justice. His outlook broadened, in addition to his
primary emphasis on spiritual and religious concerns, to include
a public discourse that became bolder, that encompassed military
and global issues.

Let us look back to King's early years. It is firmly accepted that
he based his theological views chiefly on his Christian upbringing:

> The church has always been a second home for me. As far
> back as I can remember I was in the church every Sunday.
> I guess this was inevitable since my father was the pastor

of my church, but I never regretted going to church until I passed through a state of skepticism in my second year of college. My best friends were in Sunday school, and it was in Sunday school that helped me build the capacity for getting along with people."[6]

That getting along with people as King said, ultimately translated into an incalculable concern for people and the quality of their lives. He saw each person as an individual with inherent and inalienable human value—so much so that he risked everything to free a nation and its people from racial degradation and its accompanying violence. He lived out the truth of scripture, "no one has greater love than this, to lay down one's life for one's friends." (John 15:13, NRSV).

According to King biographer Lewis Baldwin, one of the teachings King heard from his father was on the sacredness of humanity.[7] What he heard reinforced what he believed on the Christian doctrine that men are "created in the image and likeness of God." This single conviction of Dr. King is the complex principle at the center of his public ministry and his global outreach that must be understood to fully understand the man and his philosophy. As a young lad, King had often observed his father's courage in confronting those who would challenge his humanity and self-respect. On one occasion, a traffic policeman spoke in a disrespectful and degrading manner to his father, using the traditional demeaning salutation, "boy"! Daddy King quickly responded, pointing to his son Mike [Martin] who was with him at the time, "that's a boy, I'm a man."[8] he demanded respect, and this demand for respect was clearly illustrated during a most memorable incident "when a shoe clerk declined to serve him unless he and his father moved to the rear of the store. 'We'll either buy shoes sitting here or we won't buy any shoes at all,' his father growled, and he marched Mike toward the door."[9] These kinds of inhumane encounters were common place seeing that King grew up in Atlanta's southern culture of segregation and dehumanization. "The Ku Klux Klan and other racist elements were visibly present, and black Atlantans suffered emotionally and physically from the daily routine of abusive language and mistreatment."[10] It was King's parent's example, who exemplified moral and spiritual character as well as their traditional religious cultural values which provided a sure foundation and secure environment for him to grow and learn in. his father was very active in civil rights in Atlanta. Daddy King had served as president of the NAACP in Atlanta. He was considered a social reformer who refused to ride the city bus after observing an attack on black passengers. He also took a leadership role in the fight on behalf of fair salaries for teachers.[11] King observed his father in the role of pastor of the Ebenezer Baptist church, one of the most successful congregations in Atlanta.

In addition to his emphasis on spiritual and religious values in his life and ministry; it was in fact, the spiritual ethos of the black church and its leadership—watching his father front and center in the struggle for the rights of black people—that helped to ground Martin Luther King, Jr. in his essential values of social justice.

King lived during the controversial era of American life before civil rights, and came of age in his leadership during the formative social atmosphere during groundbreaking civil rights pushes in the United States. The impact of the struggle for civil rights required him to give the most of himself. This period merged with his spiritual experiences, beliefs and Christian upbringing. His exposure to preachers whose natural oratorical gifts provided and incubator for his own gifted oratory helped give full expression to his eloquence when eventually leaders called upon him to lead the Civil Rights Movement.

The gifted speech-making of Howard Thurman, the passionate preaching of Mordecai Johnson, the enchanting homiletical savvy of Benjamin Mays, and so many others impacted his preaching and life greatly. What Martin Luther King, Jr. understood about his life, social justice, the need for human equality, the lives of other people, and the deeply diverse spectrum of humanity spilled out from the truncations of its imbedded roots when he preached. The unlikely nexus of these events provided the unique platform upon which he built his enormous and effective body of thought, social and religious public-speaking.

Year after year, the words of the Bible and a generational pattern of preaching filled King's life. As the prism through which his own preaching and speechifying developed, the Holy Scriptures sourced the profound worldview that informed his work. Upon King's completion of his formal education, his desire was to live out what he believed to be his true calling, a pastor in his family tradition. Though Martin Luther King, Jr. may have had, from the beginning, a glimpse of his personal destiny; he may have had in his heart the eternal destiny of where his life would lead him; still, one wonders if he could have ever realized an appointment with history and posterity such as did await him. If not in American history, he was certainly the best orator of the twentieth century. In 1954, when he left Atlanta to travel to Montgomery Alabama to preach his first sermon at the Dexter Avenue Baptist Church, he was aware of God's inspiration in his preaching abilities. Obviously he wanted to do well seeing that this prestigious pulpit was vacant and in need of a pastor. This sermon would be his formal introduction and trial presentation before the congregation. King said,

> That Saturday evening as I began going over my sermon, I was aware of a certain anxiety. Although I had preached many times before—having served as associate pastor of my father's church in Atlanta for four years, and having done all of the preaching there for three successive summers—I was very conscious this time that I was on trial. How could I best impress the congregation? Since the membership was educated and intelligent, should I attempt to interest it with a display of scholarship? Or should I preach just as I had always done, depending finally on the inspiration of the spirit of God? I decided to follow the latter course. I said to myself, "Keep Martin Luther King in the background and God in the foreground and everything will be all right. Remember you are a channel of the gospel and not the source.[12]

King's message was well received by the Dexter congregation. His sermon topic: "The Three Dimensions of a Complete life." The following brief excerpt from this sermon reveals King's captivating and creative preaching ability:

> Man is God's marvelous creation, crowned with glory and honor, and because of this you can't quite hem him in. you can put him in Bedford's prison, but somehow his mind will break out through the bars to scratch a *Pilgrim's Progress* across the pages of history. you can bring him down in his wretched old age, with his body broken down and his vision all but gone, and yet in the form of a Handel, he will look up and imagine that he hears the very angels singing, and he will come back and scratch across the pages of history a "Hallelujah Chorus. This is Man. He is God's marvelous creation. Through his mind he can leap oceans, break through walls, and transcend the categories of time and space. The stars may be marvelous, but not so marvelous as the mind of man that comprehended them."[13]

Within a month after preaching his sermon at the Dexter church, King received a letter from the Pulpit selection Committee stating that he had been unanimously called to the pastorate of the Dexter avenue Baptist Church.[14] There were other job possibilities for King, including two churches in the northeast, New York, Massachusetts and teaching and administration positions in academia.[15] However, it was a widely known fact that King's heart was in the south. Of the south he said, "The south, after all, was our home. Despite its shortcomings we loved it as home, and had a real desire to do something about the problems that we had felt as youngsters. We never wanted to be considered detached spectators."[16]

King had intended to simply take his Kingdom message to the people of Dexter Baptist church who needed to refocus their vision beyond the status quo of the black elite social class and culture of Montgomery. On the other hand, the Dexter church also wanted to recover from the previous bombastic highly contentious pastor Vernon Johns, of whom the church could hardly temper. in fact, longtime Dexter church Clerk R. D. Nesbitt, member of the pulpit search committee remarked "What he [the church] needed, was a more traditional pastor—an educated and trained one, to be sure, in the Dexter tradition, but someone more conventional than Johns in dress, manner, and behavior, someone less controversial, perhaps a younger and less established man who could not give the deacons such a battle."[17] however, following the arrest of Rosa Parks who refused to give up her seat on the bus to a white man on December 1, 1955, King found himself at the head of one of the most social transformative movements of the 20th century. He was literally caught off guard by the suggestion that he should be the president of this new organization, The Montgomery Improvement Association. King said, "The action had caught me unawares. It had happened so quickly that I did not even have time to think it through. It is probable that if I had, I would have declined the nomination."[18] On the night of December 5, 1955, his first speech in this new role reflected again the creative rhetorical imagination of the young preacher. The address given at the Holt Street Baptist Church was from a minister who had less than one hour to prepare and put together his speech, he spoke with substance, eloquence and passion saying:

> We are here this evening for serious business. We are here in a general sense because first and foremost we are American citizens and we are determined to apply our citizenship to the fullness of its meaning. We are here also because of our love for democracy, because of our deep-seated belief that democracy transformed from thin paper to thick action is the greatest form of government on earth.
>
> You know, my friends, there comes a time when people get tired of being trampled over by the iron feet of oppression. There comes a time, my friends, when people get tired of being plunged across the abyss of humiliation, where they

experience the bleakness of nagging despair. There comes a time when people get tired of being pushed out of the glittering sunlight of life's July, and left standing amid the piercing chill of an alpine November.

And we are not wrong. We are not wrong in what we are doing. If we are wrong, the Supreme Court of this nation is wrong. If we are wrong, the Constitution of the United States is wrong. If we are wrong God almighty is wrong. If we are wrong, Jesus of Nazareth was merely a utopian dreamer that never came down to earth. And we are determined here in Montgomery to work and fight until Justice runs down like water and righteousness like a mighty stream.

I want to say that in all of our actions we must stick together. Unity is the great need of the hour, and if we are united we can get many things that we not only desire but which we justly deserve. And because we are doing it within the law. There is never a time in our American democracy that we must ever think we're wrong when we protest. We reserve that right.[19]

Biographer Taylor Branch captures the tone of the moment, saying "King paused. The church was quiet but it was humming."[20] The congregation eagerly expecting a Word of hope for such a time as this. And King would deliver, continuing on saying:

We, the disinherited of this land, we who have been oppressed so long, are tired of going through the long night of captivity. And now we are reaching out for the daybreak of freedom and justice and equality. May I say to you, my friends, as I come to a close…that we must keep…God in the forefront. Let us be Christian in all of our actions. But I want to tell you this evening that it is not enough for us to talk about love. Love is one of the pivotal points of the Christian faith. There is another side called justice.

Standing beside love is always justice and we are only using the tool of justice. Not only are we using the tool of persuasion but we've come to see that we've got to use the tools of coercion. Not only is this thing a process of education but it is also a process of legislation.

As we stand and sit here this evening and as we prepare ourselves for what lies ahead, let us go out with a grim and bold determination that we are going to stick together. We are going to work together. Right here in Montgomery, when the history books are written in the future, somebody will have to say, "There lived a race of people, a black people, 'fleecy locks and black complexion,' a people who had the moral courage to stand up for their rights. And thereby they injected a new meaning into the veins of history and of civilization.[21]

Few prominent preachers, black or otherwise, have ever achieved the pulpit status and dynamic of Martin Luther King. Upon study, his skill of effectively blending the demands of homiletics and ecclesiology, revealed his enormous stature as a preacher. His abilities transformed the Civil Rights Movement. His leadership, under the requirements of the movement and its endeavors, accompanied with his exceptional preaching; fully understood and appreciated only when viewed as threads of the spectrum out of which it grew.

King established a precise and rich, textured and resonant preaching style that moved people everywhere. In later years of his growth and development, the essential formulation of his experiences and his ideas propelled him, along with the black church, forward in matters of social justice to national and international significance. As such, for his country and for his family of a wife and four children, for human history, the language of freedom, liberty, respect and restoration of the human spirit, its worth, in every possible sphere of human activity, defined not only King's preaching, but also his ecclesiology.

Not surprisingly, under the leadership of Dr. King, the character of the black church underwent a major shift specifically in 1955 with Rosa Parks and the events surrounding the Montgomery Bus

Boycott. Wisely, he seized the moment of this event to launch the larger forum of the Civil Rights Movement. Simple yet profound in its social, political and historical aspect; perhaps for the first time since its founding under Richard Allen and Absalom Jones in 1760, the black church realized an expansion in the purpose of its own spiritual and social trajectory. In 1955, the black church went from being a vibrant spiritual safe haven for blacks to a mighty force with which America had finally to reckon.

Today, the complete social impact of the black Church in America is still to be fully determined. Appreciated for centuries for lively spirituals, gospel music, and the animated preaching it produced, these very same traditions have been strong underpinnings in and influences upon American church and popular culture. And with Dr. King now so visible in black church life, seemingly, he forged a new definition of the black church during the 1950's and 1960's. A definition firmly immersed in social justice and activism. King's tenet belief in the worth and dignity of all individuals propelled him to develop a compelling preaching style, its language so transcendent, it reached far beyond the boundaries and cultural concerns of the black church. His approach to preaching emerged and has survived as an art form that was itself an untraditional and mesmerizing component of an already lively tradition of black ecclesiology.

Without question, King's preaching transformed the traditional Sunday morning "feel good" haven into a lively change agent. It was to a society polarized for centuries by racial discrimination, acceptance of unfair labor practices, and a strident complacency about the consequences which had barred them from meaningful economic participation or parity in all of American life. Embodied in the King sermons were life giving assurances to oppressed black people in particular and oppressed people in general. It pricked the conscience of African Americans to shake off complacency and to shake up their society. With his sermons, he created a complex relationship between himself and his text and between his text and his audience. His text conveyed with unmistakable clarity to his audience that he understood their hopes and fears, their struggles and triumphs. Then, from a jail house cell, his homily in a letter: *Letter from the Birmingham Jail*, challenged a recalcitrant white clergy, largely disinterested in matters of social justice and racial equality, to accept accountability for their enablement of racial violence and injustice.

Despite his mentoring by the preaching tradition of elders of the black church, Martin Luther King's sermons also loosely reflected a moving acquaintance and understanding of the dialogues and homiletic concerns of his contemporaries. King's sermons reveal moments of intense personal reflection, passionately peppered often with anecdotes of his own personal experiences. For example:

> Due to my involvement in the struggle for the freedom of my people, I have known very few quiet days in the last few years. I have been imprisoned in Alabama and Georgia jails twelve times. My home has been bombed twice. A day seldom passes that my family and I are not the recipients of threats of death. I have been the victim of a near-fatal stabbing. So in a real sense I have been battered by the storms of persecution.[22]

The turbulence that surrounded King's activism did not muddle the texts of his sermons. They were not words needlessly spent on trepidations and bitter sorrows. They demonstrated that he knew first-hand the horrors of black people. They were his horrors, too. Fearless and forceful and confrontational, he put his sermons to hearers in a willing congregation and to unwilling hearers of a society in a great nation he knew had yet to fulfill its potential and obligations to all its constituents. Ever the sword that pierced, King's words tore the veil of human activity and plumed the depths of human motivation: "I submit to you that if a man hasn't discovered something he will die for, he isn't fit to live."[23] empathetic and constructed to console his supporters, his words highlighted concerns about a social infrastructure so corrupt, it daily presented numerous nearly insurmountable barriers that defied his adherents to go on living. King's sermons took the highest moral ground—yet; they were entirely open and accessible to those who had an ear to hear.

From within, the lines between the black church as a sacred and social institution, were finely drawn. The black church he felt; just like the nation, had not yet reached its fullest potential. He thought the church was feeble—too frail. "So often," he wrote, "The contemporary Church is a weak, ineffectual voice with an uncertain sound. So often it is an arch defender of the status quo." This stark and honest opinion is evidence that as much as the black church had nurtured him, he wanted to nurture it with "tough love." he was not blind to the flaws and foibles of the black church; hence, it was not isolated from the criticisms he clearly intended as encouragement for the church to rise to the occasion of its highest potential in its finest moment. King's confidence in the people and the latent potentials of the black church was never in doubt.

What can be said of this community today—this gathering of believers in Christ, which calls itself with great pride, the family of God? Has it continued to grow since the days of the Civil Rights Movement? Is there still this need for social activism? If so, forty years after the death of Dr. Martin Luther King, does it have the courage to do today what it did yesterday? Interestingly, Jesus asks in Mark's Gospel this question: "Who is my mother, brother or sister, but they that do the will of my Father" (Mark 3:35). William Barclay in his commentary on Mark says, "Jesus lays down the conditions of true kinship. It is not solely a matter of flesh and blood."[24] in order to be a true family, one and all must commit to doing God's will. God's will to be done on earth as it is done in heaven. N.T. Wright suggests that "God's passion for justice must become our passion for justice."[25]

Fifty years ago the issues seemed much clearer, blacks could not vote in America's democracy, but they can do so today. Fifty years ago blacks could not sit and eat or live where they chose, but for the most part today they can do so if they have found a reasonable measure of economic justice. if not for those fighters of freedom who sought to do God's will and fight against injustice, the narrow structure of America's pre-Civil Rights society, intended to benefit only one segment of its population would still be in place. The Civil Rights Movement of the 50's and 60's demonstrated how the church can be the catalyst for social and economic change. When Jesus tells the story of the Good Samaritan in Luke 10:30—37, he is speaking not of church buildings and organizations, but about the fact that those who take his words seriously can truly make substantive change in the world. The good works of them that do the will of God make known his son Jesus to others not yet prone to do his will. Dr. King's legacy proves it is not enough simply to be aware of the issues. To directly address religious corruption and social ills that lead to social injustice is what Jesus did, and in doing the same, Martin Luther King, Jr. practiced doing the will of God. Today, the authentic Christian Church must mobilize and continue to validate struggles for truth and social justice where ever there is a need to do so—to make a difference in people's lives and to seek to repair the damage and brokenness that result from social injustice.

CHAPTER THREE

New Leadership, New Voice, Same Vision

✳

"To those of my race who depend on bettering their condition in a foreign land or who underestimate the importance of cultivating friendly relations with the Southern white man, who is their next door neighbor, I would say, 'cast down your bucket where you are.'"[143] *Booker T. Washington*

MARTIN LUTHER KING, JR. was a student of history; he had studied other approaches to social reform relative to race relations in America. He said of social change "that no revolution can take place without a methodology suited to the circumstances of the period."[144] King's critique of other early twentieth century black leaders such as Booker T. Washington, W. E. B. Du Bois, and Marcus Garvey, reveal both his appreciation for their contributions, as well as his keen awareness of the limitations of the various methods and approaches to social reform employed by these leaders in their quest for freedom in America. No doubt, King could have directed his words from the Birmingham Jail to the accommodationist

Booker T. Washington, when he said, "For years now I have heard the word 'Wait!' it rings in the ear of every Negro with piercing familiarity. This 'Wait' has almost always meant 'never.' We must come to see, with one of our distinguished jurists, that 'justice too long delayed is justice denied.'"[145]

Washington's philosophy of "Casting down your buckets where you are" was viewed by King as not doing enough to exact real meaningful and lasting social reform. "The dark days following the period of Reconstruction were times where people were to be content, he said in effect, with doing well what times permit you to do at all. However, this path, they soon felt, had too little freedom in its present and too little promise in its future."[146] Booker T. Washington's philosophy was fashioned and crafted from the mind of his mentor. In 1872, at the age of sixteen, Booker T. arrived on the campus of Hampton Institute, "a school molded from the ideas of practical education of its founder, Samuel Chapman Armstrong. Armstrong taught his students that labor was a 'spiritual force, that physical work not only increased wage-earning capacity but promoted fidelity, accuracy, honesty, persistence, and intelligence."[147] Washington became a passionate exponent of Armstrong's ideology and was thereby convinced that the greatest hope for blacks must be found in providing useful service and production of what the white community wanted. in advising those of his race, he admonished: "To those of my race who depend upon bettering their condition in a foreign land or who underestimate the importance of cultivating friendly relations with the southern white man…I would say 'Cast down your bucket where you are'—cast it down in making friends in every manly way of the people of all races by whom we are surrounded. Cast it down in agriculture, in mechanics, in commerce, in domestic service…"[148]

In a speech given by Washington in 1884 on *Racial Harmony and Black Progress*, he said "Brains, property, and character for the negro will settle the question of civil rights. The best course to pursue in regard to the civil rights bill in the south is to let it alone; let it alone and it will settle itself."[149] Washington believed that overtime, and with patience, whites would come to accept blacks if they saw them as worthwhile contributors to the economic system. "White southerners liked Washington's relative disinterest in political and civil rights for negroes. They liked the way in which he placed confidence in the southern whites regarding their good treatment of blacks who proved themselves to be useful, law-abiding citizens."[150] While King valued the virtues associated with "brains, property ownership and character" his approach to social reform involved political engagement through legislative actions that would force real systemic changes in the political structure of this nation. King voiced the need for a just legislative bill: "it is a simple matter of justice that America, in dealing creatively with the task of raising the Negro from backwardness, should also be rescuing a large stratum of forgotten white poor. A Bill of Rights for the Disadvantaged could mark the rise of a new era..."[151] While Armstrong taught his students that labor was a "spiritual force" King, sought to convince the world that Justice and righteousness are the true "spiritual force".

King admired W. E. B. Du Bois, a highly respected, twentieth century Harvard trained social historian who contributed significantly to African American intellectual understanding and thought. King remarked: "as early as 1906 W. E. B. Du Bois's prophesied that 'the problem of the twentieth century will be the problem of the color line.' Now as we stand two-thirds into this existing period in history we know full well that racism is still that hound of hell which dogs the tracks of our civilization."[152] Du Bois philosophy is in many ways an exact opposition to that of Booker T. Washington's views on race relations. King was mindful of the tension that existed between these two black leaders. Du Bois "accused Washington of preaching a 'gospel of Work and Money to such an extent as apparently almost completely to overshadow the higher aims of life.'"[153] on the other hand, "Washington believed that the Negro, starting with so little, would have to work up gradually before he could attain a position of power and respectability in the south."[154] King stated that, "Dr. W.E.B. Dubois, in his earlier years at the turn of the century, urged the 'Talented tenth' to rise and pull behind it the masses of the race. His doctrine served somewhat to counteract the apparent resignation of Booker T. Washington's philosophy. Yet, in the very nature of Du Bois's outlook there was no role for the whole people."[155] King believed the very concept of the "talented tenth" did not take into account the 90 percent who may not be as talented. According to Cornel West's, critique of Du Bois, West said, "in style and substance, a proud black man of letters primarily influenced by nineteenth-century Euro-American traditions."[156] West asserts, "Du Bois's enlightenment worldview—his first foundation—prohibited this kind of understanding. Instead, he adopted a mild elitism that underestimated the capacity of everyday people to 'know' about life.[157] The elitist views of Du Bois philosophy would be tested and challenged.

By 1948 Du Bois had critiqued his Talented tenth supposition, clearly rethinking the validity of his own proposal. He stated: 'I realized that it was quite possible that my plan of training a talented tenth might put in control and power, a group of selfish, self-indulgent, well-to-do men, whose basic interest in solving the negro Problem was personal; personal freedom and unhampered enjoyment and use of the world, without any real care, or certainly no arousing care, as to what became of the mass of American Negroes, or of the mass of any people.'[158] Feminist social critic bell hooks writes, "Growing up in the fifties, I was acutely aware of the contempt black folks with class privilege directed toward the masses."[159]

In Du Bois's "The Talented Tenth Memorial address delivered at the nineteenth Grand Boulé Conclave, sigma Pi Phi gathering, he attempted to expand his earlier Talented Tenth theory by calling for a new Talented Tenth. According to Du Bois what was needed was an alliance with culture groups from Europe, Asia and Africa. "Such organization calls for more than a tenth of our number. One one-hundredth or thirty thousand persons are indicated, with directing council composed of educated and specially trained experts in the main branches of science and the main categories of human work, and a paid executive committee of five or six persons to carry out the program."[160]

The new Talented Tenth reflected the same elitist's characteristics as the earlier version yet on a grander scale. Du Bois decided that America would never become the nation he'd envision and gave up his citizenship moving to Ghana. "In the end, Du Bois's enlightenment worldview, Victorian strategies, and American optimism failed him. He left America in militant despair—the very despair he had avoided earlier—and mistakenly hoped for the rise of a strong postcolonial and united Africa.[161]

King's Christian ethic was in conflict with the concept of the talented tenth motif. The teachings of Jesus, on who is the greatest in the kingdom of God, points toward a servant, childlike faith. "...The disciples came to Jesus and asked, 'Who is the greatest in the kingdom of heaven?' He called a child, whom he put among them, and said, 'Truly I tell you, unless you change and become like children, you will never enter the kingdom of heaven." (Matthew 18:1—2 NRSV). King also alluded to this theme in the sermon he preached from the pulpit of Ebenezer Baptist Church, February 4, 1968. The sermon, entitled "a Drum Majors instinct." he used the scripture passage from Mark's gospel in which Jesus addresses the ambition mind-set of two of his disciples, James and John and their desire to sit one, on the right hand, and the other on the left hand in Christ glorious kingdom in heaven. Toward the end of the passage, Jesus would tell them, "...But whoever wishes to become great among you must be your servant, and whoever wishes to be first among you must be slave of all." (Mark 10:43—44). King said that what James and John had was a drum majors instinct. And he said we all have this innate instinct, the need to be out front, the need to lead the parade. King said that Jesus gave a new definition or norm of greatness. "If you want to be great—wonderful, but recognize that he who is greatest among you shall be your servant. That's the new definition of greatness. And this morning, the thing that I like about it...by giving that definition of greatness, it means that everybody can be great."[162] Du Bois's enlightenment "Talented tenth" motif does not square well with the humble servant model of universal greatness. Writer bell hooks asserts "a thriving, corrupt 'Talented tenth' have not only emerged as the power brokers preaching individual liberalism and black capitalism to everyone (especially the black masses), their biggest commodity is 'selling blackness.'"[163] she argues that the black elite have used their class privilege to exploit the masses of black folk. "Nowadays, practically every public representation of blackness is created by black folks who are materially privileged. More often than not they speak about the black poor and working class but not with them, or on their behalf."[164]

Perhaps the most radical of all approaches regarding a black response to dehumanization and discrimination in the quest for freedom in America was made by the Jamaican born Marcus Garvey. In 1914 he organized the Universal Negro Improvement Association. "Two years later he came to the united states to organize a New York chapter of the UNIA. At the end of the war the association grew rapidly, and according to its leader there were more than thirty branches by the middle of the 1919."[165] Marcus Garvey is best known for his back to Africa Movement. "Garvey said that the only hope for Negro Americans was to flee America and return to Africa and build up a country of their own."[166] Garvey gained great popularity and his following among the poor black masses out-numbered the members in Du Bois's organization, the N.A.A.C.P. "Despite their vigorous efforts, the national association for the advancement of Colored People and the Commission on interracial Cooperation failed to reach more than a small minority of blacks and whites; and although it succeeded in achieving ends that were beneficial to all negroes, it failed to capture the imagination and secure the following of the masses."[167] Due to Garvey's efforts, he "appealed to the League of Nations for permission to settle a colony in Africa and opened negotiations with Liberia. In 1923, Garvey's plans were derailed when he was charged with "using the mail to defraud in raising money for his steamship line. He was found guilty, and two years later entered the Atlanta penitentiary to serve a five-year term."[168] he was later deported permanently from the US.

Garvey's nationalist philosophy continued to live on through the work of other nationalist thinkers like, Elijah Muhammad. He was born Elijah Poole from Sandersville, Georgia on October 7, 1897. He is considered the original leader of the lost Found Black nation of Islam. "Elijah learned what he knew of Islam from a shadowy, mysterious evangelist who went by a variety of aliases, but who was most popularly known as Wali Farrad, or Wallace Fard. Fard claimed to have come from the Holy City of Mecca on a mission of redemption and restoration of the Black under caste."[169] Malcolm X and Louis Farrakhan followed in the tradition of the Black Nation of Islam. Of course Malcolm X upon his return from Mecca, revised his thinking regarding the separatist ideology of the Black Nation of Islam organization, broke away to start his own movement shortly before his assassination in 1965.

King's response to Marcus Garvey's approach to social reform is not surprising. King believed that Garvey touched upon an emotional chord amongst blacks who rejected concepts of inferiority. King said, "There was reason to be proud of their heritage as well as their bitterly won achievements in America. yet his plan was doomed because an exodus to Africa in the twentieth century by a people who had struck roots for three and a half centuries in the new World did not have the ring of progress."[170] Garvey's approaches to freedom, from the oppressive conditions in America were extremely unrealistic and unappealing to the masses of blacks in this country.

Having examined the approaches of Washington, Du Bois, and Garvey, the question then is what made Martin Luther King's appeal to racial reconciliation and social reform more effective than other reformers of the twentieth century? Generally speaking, King was able to combine a synthesis of spiritual, intellectual and emotional aspects in his approach to confronting not only the race issue, but other issues of injustice in America. These areas: ethos of faith, the logos of fact, and the Pathos of feeling provide a framework for observing the voice, vision and message of Martin Luther King for contemporary society.

First, King was aware of the spiritual nature of the battle over the issue of race and he did not resist the spiritual ethos of his faith tradition. King, said, "Even more vital in the Negro's resistance to violence was the force of his deeply rooted spiritual belief."[171] The awareness and the willingness to acknowledge the role of faith in the revolution to overcome racial discrimination was more than a novel idea but a moral conviction. Mark Noll suggests that the three-fold nature of understanding what African American Religion meant to the contemporary history:

> First, the intellectual sophisticated convictions of educated leaders like Martin Luther King, Jr., represented a compound of many elements. Second, the social sophisticated convictions of such leaders were matched and balanced by the pre-critical beliefs of many civil rights foot soldiers who religion remained close to the elemental faiths of the nineteenth century. Third, the particular history of African-American thought explains why the faith that drove the civil rights movement differed markedly from other varieties of American religion.[172]

King understood the very nature of the civil rights movement rested on the back of the black church tradition. In speaking about the Montgomery Bus Boycott, he said, "The negro church had emerged with increasing impact in the civil-rights struggle. Negro ministers, with a growing awareness that the true witness of a Christian life is the projection of a social gospel, had accepted leadership in the fight for racial justice."[173] Introducing the ethos of Christian faith into movement allowed King to more readily use the Christian scriptures to navigate the sensitive American landscape on the issue of Race. One cannot deny the variety of hues; shades of colors within the human tapestry that the Creator chose to assemble on His planet. In fact, a tremendous appreciation for such a vast diversity is in order. As the Psalmist declared:

When I look at your heavens, the work of your fingers, the moon and the stars that you have established; what are human beings that you are mindful of them, mortals' that you care for them? Yet you have made them a little lower than angels, and crowned them with glory and honor." (Psalms 8:3—5)

In King's book "The Measure of a Man" he opened chapter one with the question: "What is man?" Then he postulates a reckoning with the answer and writes based on Psalm 8:

One day the psalmist looked up and noticed the vastness of the cosmic order. He noticed the vastness of the cosmic order. he noticed the infinite expanse of the solar system; he noticed the beautiful stars; he gazed at the moon with all its scintillating beauty, and he said in the midst of all this, "what is man?" he comes forth with an answer: "Thou hast made him a little lower than the angels, and crowned him with glory and honor." Godspeed, Moffatt, and the Revised standard would say, "Thou hast made him a little less than divine, a little less than God, and crowned him with glory and honor." it is this realistic position that I would like to use as a basis of our thinking together and our meditation on the question "What is man?"[174]

In King's use of this passage, it points toward a post-racial society. It is not unusual to hear people speak of living in an America which is colorblind, where race no longer matters. Though this kind of expression or sentiment may be well intentioned, such sentiment's often falls short of the realities incumbent upon human existence and interaction. Being "colorblind" is not necessarily a productive linguistic vehicle to navigate the racial landscape filled with historical as well as contemporary racial and cultural differences and social complexities. For a society to pursue color-blindness as a basis of racial healing and reconciliation is to completely miss out on the majestic beauty of God's purpose and order. Nevertheless, I believe what King hoped for is that our nation would come to see all people as being created in the image of God. This would mean that

America would enter into a "post-racial" era where the significance of race as an arbitrator of human worth, dignity and value will no longer have the same power as it had up to half of the twentieth century and now into the twenty-first century. A true "post-racial society" will bring America ever so close to the realization and manifestation of King's noble idea where men [women] would be finally judged not by the color of their skin but by the content of the character.

Shelby Steele in his recent work, "A Bound Man: Why We Are Excited About Obama and Why He Can't Win" reflects this subtle change. Millions of Americans from all walks of life were elated that Steele was wrong in his analysis of Barack Obama's likelihood of becoming America's first African American president, and the dramatic outcome of the 2008 presidential race. Contrary to the title of Steele's book, Obama won! Steele says of Obama:

> He is interesting for not fitting into old racial conventions. Not only does he stand in stark contrast to a black leadership with which Americans of all races have grown exhausted— the likes of Al Sharpton, Jesse Jackson, and Julian Bond—he embodies something that no other presidential candidate possibly can: the idealism that race is but a negligible human difference. Here is the radicalism, innate to his pedigree, which automatically casts him as the perfect antidote to America's corrosive racial politics. After all, this is the radicalism by which Martin Luther King put Americans in touch—if only briefly—with their human universality.[175]

Yet, at the dawn of the twenty-first century, still America lingers in a veritable dense fog of complacency of racial progress. The second element that differentiates King's approach has to do with the logos of fact. As king said, social change and the methods must be suited to the circumstances of the period. Prophetically, he envisioned a "post-racial" society. In fact, it is this kind of society in which King dreamed of and fought for. This post-racial society may owe its victory in large measure, not only to the battles waged during the Civil Rights Era, but as well to one of the outcomes of Civil Rights legislation: the large number of immigrants who have since the 50's and 60's made America their home. Many Hispanics, Latinos from Central and South America now make up the largest minority group in America. The 2005 Census Bureau reports that Hispanics accounted for nearly half of the U.S. population growth during the period July 1, 2004—July 1, 2005. The Hispanic population increased by 1.3 million during that period. according to this same Census Bureau Report, as of 2005 "Hispanics comprise 42.7 million, blacks including African Americans and more recently arrived Africans and blacks of Caribbean origin, total 39.7 million."[176] With minority groups now constituting one-third of the total American population, the way in which race is viewed or even talked about, is uniquely different than the way it was viewed or talked about prior to, and during the Civil Rights era of the 50's and 60's. in fact, in data released in 2007 Census Bureau shows that the nation's minority population has reached a new milestone, surpassing 100 million, and accounting for one in three U.S. residents.[177] it must be understood that prior to the 60s the racialization of the two main racial population groups was the major social stratification of America life. The historical tapestry of America was in black and white, it is not so today!

Finally, King was able to tap into the pathos of feeling; the emotional aspects of King's ministry through the sound and substance of his message cannot be denied. As a gifted preacher King knew what moved his audience intellectually and emotionally. As Baldwin suggest, "Much of King's genius was evident in the fact that he could preach effectively to any audience, black or white, with confidence and ease."[178] Biographer David L. Lewis summed it up in the following: "He was the echo chamber of the racially oppressed but an echo chamber whose reverberations were rounder, more intelligible, and much more polite than the raw cries that it transformed."[179] King represented a new kind of leadership as well as a new voice, yet his vision for freedom and equality was as persistent as those freedom fighters who had come before him.

CHAPTER FOUR

Evangelical Liberalism: Justice is a social Collaboration

—— ✳ ——

"There are always primary contracts between the weak and the strong, the privileged and the underprivileged, but they are generally contracts within zones of agreement which leave the status of the individual intact."[38] *Howard Thurman*

EVANGELICAL CHRISTIANITY HISTORICALLY HAS committed its mission to preaching the Gospel of Jesus Christ and propagating the message of God's eternal salvation for the human soul. However, with this traditionally singular focus on salvation; a gulf has existed between the Church's conception of personal salvation and the social responsibility required of each individual to ensure that all human beings have a sustainable environment of peace and reconciliation in which to live out salvation. That isn't to say that life in the lord is without conflict; nonetheless, without an uncompromised framework of peace and reconciliation, life and the human experience fall well below God's intention of a full life lived now along with the hopeful expectation of the life promised to come.

Martin Luther King, Jr.'s personal theology intersected at this crucial juncture. His embrace of liberal evangelicalism held that a peaceful society and a just society is God's will for all humanity. He believed in personal universality and preached that every person should be able to express the total worth of their human dignity without the obstruction of unjust social assemblages. Those who chose to have a personal relationship with God through Jesus Christ, to seek fullness of life, had the right to freely respond to God; to seek this precious reciprocal bond of unity and wholeness. This can happen only in a completely just and humane society.

While in Birmingham in April of 1963, Dr. King gave his rationale for joining the cause of justice.

> I am in Birmingham because injustice is here. Just as the prophets of the eighth Century B.C. left their villages and carried their 'thus saith the Lord' far beyond the boundaries of their hometowns, and just as the Apostle Paul left his village of Tarsus and carried the Gospel of Jesus Christ to the far corners of the Greco Roman world, so am I compelled to carry the gospel of freedom beyond my own hometown. Like Paul, I must constantly respond to the Macedonian call for aid.[39]

As an evangelical preacher, King was interested in preaching the Gospel of Jesus Christ in its purest unvarnished form stripped down to the truth: he believed the scriptures which say "...for those who do not love a brother or sister whom they have seen, cannot love God whom they have not seen." (I John 4:20 NRSV). In communicating the Gospel in this way, it reminded his hearers of the destructiveness of social injustice and spiritual hypocrisy. On the one hand, he fought for social justice for all men, women and children; and on the other, attempted desperately to dissuade all Christians—black, white and other, of the deception, perils and comforts of practicing false religion. King maintained that without peaceful confrontation as he practiced, equal rights might never become a reality for black, poor and otherwise oppressed citizens of the United States. Even though he was roundly accused of being a trouble-maker, he stood by his use of direct, non-violent confrontation as a way of illuminating the injustices of segregation and the Jim Crow laws that supported it. He believed that human rights and the need for everyone to be able to wholly express their humanity superseded unjust laws—that God-given inalienable rights took precedence over injustice. King said that, "one who breaks such laws must do it openly, lovingly," that such a person shows greater respect for laws by demanding they be just.

For example, when King preached from Luke's Gospel on the Prodigal son, he enlarged that message beyond its traditional interpretation of the young man who returned home broken after wasteful living. The Prodigal son was indeed beaten down and abandoned by a hostile world. Fortunately for him, he was able to return to a loving father eager to forgive him, and he was received back into the family. King saw the story differently, and applied his interpretation this way:

> This is the glory of our religion: that when man decides to rise up from his mistakes, from his sin, from his evil, there is a loving God saying, "Come home, I still love you." Oh, I can hear voices crying out today saying to Western civilization: you strayed away to the far country of colonialism and imperialism. You have trampled over one billion six hundred million of your colored brothers in Africa and Asia. But, O Western Civilization, if you will come to yourself, rise up, and come back home, I will take you in. it seems that I can hear a voice saying to America: you started out right. You wrote in our Declaration of independence that 'all men are created equal and endowed by their Creator with certain inalienable rights. Among these are life, liberty, and the pursuit of happiness.' But, America, you strayed away from that sublime principle. You left the house of your great heritage and strayed away into a far country of segregation

and discrimination. You have trampled over six million of your brothers. You have deprived them of the basic goods of life. You have taken from them their self-respect and their sense of dignity. You have treated them as if they were things rather than persons. Because of this a famine has broken out in your land. In the midst of all your material wealth, you are spiritually and morally poverty-stricken, unable to speak to the conscience of this world. America, in this famine situation, if you will come to yourself and rise up and decide to come back home, I will take you in, for you are made for something high and something noble and something good.[40]

King's certainty that God stood with those in the midst of struggle for human liberty fueled his emphatic calls for freedom. in King's estimation equality, evenhandedness, and fair-mindedness were their own blueprints as perfect models for the broad based coalition needed to change this country from a race-baited society into one where coalitions between the races could be forged in order to build bridges substantial enough to sustain mutuality between the races. After all, no one planned to leave the nation in large numbers—the ideal, then, was to create every possible corridor of reason between people of every race and social background so that all could live together in dignified respect, harmony and peace. That effort of course, if earnestly embraced, would result in social and spiritual good for the entire society.

This is the kind of practical and spiritual societal logic of Dr. King which motivated his work. His driving force sought the greatest good for all, but his labor engendered him no favor. It was difficult to shatter hundreds of years of discrimination, its familiar comfort levels and the long rooted tentacle side effects on American life. Whites were accustomed to their unique and exclusive social and economic privileges, and many blacks had become medicated by that abuse and deprivation; and had resigned to merely making do. Rattling those cages of oppression brought anger and fear on the part of everyone.

King's detractors were unrelenting: blacks and whites; groups and individuals and even the United States Government. Organizations like the national association for the advancement of Colored People (NAACP), The Student Non-Violent Coordination Committee (SNCC), People United to Save Humanity (PUSH), The Congress on Racial Equality (CORE), and National Urban League (NUL) all had a vested interest in the Civil Rights Movement. They, like the Southern Christian Leadership Conference (SCLC), wanted full parity for all citizens of the United States. They each had their own strong ideas, opinions and operational strategies on how to accomplish this. No two of these organizations agreed in principal with Dr. King and his philosophy of non-violent direct action. Many of these sister organizations found his ways too *erudite*, too accommodating to the power establishment; and some thought King's approaches were forms of outright appeasement.

In 1961, Dr. J. H. Jackson, president of the National Baptist Convention, accused Martin Luther King, Jr. of causing a riot at the 81st national Baptist Convention held in Kansas City. The issue of who should next hold the presidency of the convention resulted in a fight on the platform. a delegate fell six feet from the stage to his death and for this; Jackson accused King of inciting a "militant campaign…against his own denomination and race." it was obvious that Reverend Jackson's fierce but transparent anger was directed more towards trivializing King's great national work than any complicity he may have had in an onstage brawl between two adults. Until he died, Jackson continued to blame King for the tragedy that took place at that Baptist convention at Kansas City.

In one memo from J. Edgar Hoover, who had an obsessive hate of King, he demanded to know "why the FBI had not thoroughly investigated the trouble maker King." Hoover harassed King constantly. He spied on him; wire tapped his phone, and viciously exposed some of the most private aspects of King's personal life. On January 30, 1956, danger hit even closer to home. After accepting the leadership role of the Montgomery improvement association and King's boycotting of the Montgomery Alabama Transit authority, he became the target of white hatred in the city. Taylor Branch, in *Parting the Waters*, tells what happened when King heard that his home had been bombed:

> King walked out onto the front porch. Holding up his hand for silence, he tried to still the anger by speaking with an exaggerated peacefulness in his voice. Everything was all right, he said. 'Don't get panicky. Don't do anything panicky. Don't get your weapons. If you have weapons, take them home. He who lives by the sword will perish by the sword. Remember that is what Jesus said. We are not advocating violence. We want to love our enemies. I want you to love our enemies. Be good to them. This is what we must live by. We must meet hate with love.[41]

While he lived, King's life was in constant danger from detractors who became outright adversaries like J. Edgar Hoover. His preaching brought with it mountains of criticism from every corridor of people, including that of theologians, who refused to concur with the moral mandate King used although it came straight from the Gospel of Jesus Christ.

King's preaching, combining his civil rights work sought to create an atmosphere where every possible corridor of reason between people of every race and social standing could exist. Change did not occur quickly in American institutions, but that did not deter him. His work simply made the status quo much less comfortable to sustain. Lischer said, "This young, preacher who once appealed to Billy Graham for advice was the first theological thinker since the social Gospel movement to forge a synthesis of evangelical and liberal traditions in America..."[42] To the amazement of many, when he sought the counsel of Billy Graham, the father of modern evangelicalism, Graham responded with compassion and acceptance. In many of the adverse situations faced by King, Billy Graham assisted him and did not label his work as that of an agitator. Nor did Graham consider King a communist or anti-American, as so many others had. Instead, he acknowledged that King's efforts were necessary to level the playing field for disenfranchised blacks and poor and oppressed people as a legitimate and reasonable service to the Gospel of Christ.

Benjamin Mays, former president of Morehouse College in Atlanta said:

> It must be borne in mind, however, that the tragedy in life does not lie in reaching your goal. The tragedy lies in having no goal to reach. It isn't a calamity to die with dreams unfulfilled, but it is a calamity not to dream. It is not a disaster to be unable to capture our idea, but it is a disaster to have no ideal to capture. It is not a disgrace not to reach the stars, but it is a disgrace to have no stars to reach for. Not failure, but low aim is the sin.[43]

In Billy Graham, King had a true ally. King consulted him concerning the future trajectory of the Civil Rights Movement. Dr. Graham delivered help, guidance and advice. Billy Graham's friendship, prayer and moral support of King, by 1957, earned Graham favor with blacks—so much so that he was "acquiring a reputation among [blacks] as an enlightened white fundamentalist."[44]

At a highly publicized sixty-eight night crusade at Madison square Garden, Graham invited King to deliver a prayer. It should be noted that a decade before the landmark 1964 Civil Rights act legislation was passed, Graham preached against segregated evangelical rallies; eventually, Graham personally refused to conduct segregated crusades. In Chattanooga, Tennessee, Graham himself physically removed the ropes used for dividing seating between blacks and whites during his Crusades.[45]

According to King Biographer, Taylor Branch, King actually modeled his mass meetings after those of Billy Graham, which were extremely organized and well-planned. Billy Graham had skilled organizers who spent months "compiling mailing lists, enlisting church sponsors and volunteer groups, arranging publicity campaigns and special bus routes before Graham arrived for two weeks of nightly mass meetings."[46] The models stood King in good stead for his own mass gatherings.

During the height of Dr. King's activities, Montgomery, Alabama had neither [black] owned radio stations nor widely read black newspapers. Because of the scope of the Civil Rights Movement, effective organization for large meetings and marches was extremely important for stability and credibility. At the beginning of the mass meetings that preceded the Montgomery Bus Boycott, according to King, "these twice-a-week get togethers were indispensable channels of communication."[47] These gatherings were highly organized and well-managed. These meetings also facilitated solidarity across lines of Christian denominations. In addition to Graham, King was influenced greatly by preachers like Philip Brooks. Sometimes, King borrowed from his and sermons of others, but added his own, distinctive voice and the unique experiences of African American Christians.[48] Even as he relied on their themes; clearly, his prophetic voice is what is heard as he deconstructed what he appropriated from other prophetic preachers in all the irony and hope embodied in evangelism," and in the Gospel borne from familiarity with black life. King remarked concerning those who witnessed this amazing strategy, "all joined hands in the bond of Christian love."[49] Thus the mass meetings accomplished on Monday and Thursday nights are what the Christian church had failed to accomplish on Sunday mornings.[50]

Focused slightly differently from the mission of Billy Graham's evangelism, King's thrust of social justice through civil rights, blended with principles of the love of God and were fueled by the true work of human redemption, justice and righteousness—any minor contradictions between Martin Luther King, Jr. and the philosophical and theological approach of the Modern evangelical Movement of Billy Graham were nullified by their fundamental purpose to lift people above the spiritual, moral and material degeneracy of racism.

While Billy Graham was extremely beneficent toward Martin Luther King, his favor toward the young leader was unique. Within the ranks of Southern Baptist leadership, the denomination historically resistant to speaking out against racial injustice eventually began to bring down its barriers enough to give King and his concerns an audience. One such leader was Dr. Jess Moody, founding president of Palm Beach Atlantic University in West Palm Beach, Florida. He was the former president of the Southern Baptist Pastor's Conference. Moody recalls the dinner meeting he had with King and Andrew Young in Atlantic City, New Jersey. This brief encounter took place in 1964 during a gathering of the American Baptist Convention. It was at this dinner according to Reverend Moody that Dr. King spoke to him frankly of his strong evangelical Christian convictions. King stated, "The social action that we are involved in will fail without Christ's Kingdom as its foundation."[51] Moody said he came away believing "King was thoroughly evangelical"[52] and that week King delivered a sermon entitled *Love and Forgiveness* to the American Baptist delegation.

To be evangelical is to accept without question that Jesus died for the sins of the world and that personal salvation is based upon acceptance of Jesus Christ, his death on the cross, which fulfilled his role as Redeemer of fallen humanity. King never attempted to compromise his spirituality for his cultural traditions or intellectual pedigree, and his "public, transracial ministry marked a convergence of theological scholarship and social gospel practices."[53] "With King as its voice, the Civil Rights Movement became a Word of God Movement, and the Word, exactly as it is portrayed in the new Testament, became a physical force with its own purposes and momentum."[54] It was King who insisted on including the term "Christian" in the naming of the newly formed civil rights organization, SLC the "Southern Leadership Conference. King's close friend and advisor Bayard Rustin tried to dissuade him from the idea of using the word Christian, arguing "that the new word might discourage nonreligious supporters of civil rights, but King had held firm".[55] Thusly, the name Southern "Christian" Leadership remained as the name of the most significant civil rights organization of the 50's and 60's.

It is not surprising then that King surrounded himself with preachers from many of the black Christian pulpits and churches throughout America. According to Lischer, "outside observers of SCLC and other civil rights organizations were often struck by the sheer quantity of black preachers involved in their day-to-day operations. 'SCLC is not an organization,' one of its officials told a reporter, 'it's a church.'"[56] King's Christian commitment and evangelical identity influenced his vision, voice and message, and the themes of social and legal justice that were predominant in the church organization and aided the struggle against human injustice under King's leadership. The traditional church, with spiritual leadership must face the devastation of social, economic, and political inequality in a society to achieve and equalize respect and human dignity for all people. King expressed this idea when he said:

> Religion must never overlook this and any religion that professes to be concerned about the souls of men and is not concerned about the economic conditions that damn the soul, the social conditions that corrupt men, and the city governments that cripple them, is a dry, dead, do-nothing religion in need of new blood.[57]

In other words, if the church remains silent on matters of human and social justice, where then is the moral core of existence? If social justice were left to any other interest group, what subsequently may well fall to humanity is a miscarriage of justice.

While King's theory of justice was the synthesis of many theories, his most indispensable theory was rooted in his perception of himself as a human being made worthy of a full life by God. The world around him was built upon the enduring foundation of God's love stitched together by the biblical principle of "turning the other cheek." These liberal concepts gave Dr. King both the moral and ethical covering against the harsh winds of adversity that blew upon him regularly. In response to the social climate of the mid twentieth century, King made a remarkable critique of American Christianity. Clearly frustrated that many sectors of it stood by mostly silent in the face of enormous racial strife, economic injustice, cultural and social violence, King stated that,

> The judgment of God is upon the Church. The Church has a schism in its own soul that it must close. It will be one of the tragedies of Christian history if future historians record that at the height of the twentieth century the Church was one of the greatest bulwarks of white supremacy. The Church has an opportunity and duty to lift up its voice like a trumpet and declare unto the people the immorality of segregation. It must affirm that every human life is a reflection of divinity, and that every act of injustice mars and defaces the image of God in man.[58]

The result of King's unrelenting demands on the "unjust judges" in America, for untold numbers of minorities, the doors of integration in American educational institutions began to open new economic and social opportunities not accessible prior to the 1950's. The inventive voice of Dr. Martin Luther King, Jr. and his preacher/activism was the beginning of important gains toward social and economic justice. King's impact through the events of the 1960's began to rewrite the history of American democracy.

Dr. King understood the transitory impact of poverty, illiteracy and crime—that unless the cycle were broken, people of all colors in minority communities would suffer for generations. If a person is impoverished and deprived of a means of providing for common daily needs, then circumstances might lead to the basest aspects of a person's attempt to make ends meet. To this, he said,

> As long as there is poverty in the world I can never be rich, even if I have a million dollars. As long as diseases are rampant and millions of people in this world cannot expect to live more than twenty-eight or thirty years, I can never be totally healthy even if I just got a good checkup at Mayo Clinic. I can never be what I ought to be until you are what you ought to be.[59]

Nearly a half century out, the ethnic makeup of the nation is more diverse than it has ever been in its history. Today, anyone who wants to improve their life may hope to do so without the stigma of sex, color, or nationality because of the vision, voice and message of Martin Luther King, Jr. Though the achievements related to his work are impressive, no one believes that America need yet rest on her laurels concerning racial equality and economic parity. There is still the seriousness problem of imbalanced wealth that faces every racial group; there are enormous disparities in education, and home ownership has lost its glow for everyone as the beacon of the American dream. So for many the dream voiced, still waits to be fully realized all across America, especially for those who still hold to the hope King once preached. The real influence of King's voice today will unfold as its truths are kept alive now and in the future.

Pictured on left, Dr. Jess Moody, former president of the Southern Baptist Pastor's Conference. Pictured right of Moody, Reverend Fred Shuttlesworth, Civil Rights Leader

CHAPTER FIVE

Redemptive Suffering:
Suffering Don't Last Always!

———— * ————

*"There are some things that are worse than death. To deny one's
own integrity of personality in the presence of human challenge
is one of those things."*[60] *Thurman*

KING'S PROPHETIC MESSAGE PROCLAIMED redemption. His life of
personal sacrifice is an example of the "suffering servant" and such
real and symbolic concepts of the suffering servant are permanently
rooted in the earliest Judeo Christian prophetic customs. From
Noah, to Moses, to Jeremiah, to Christ, in the depths of King's
thinking and the theology upon which he drew and built his
philosophical outlook about suffering, it was continually founded
upon the power of submission to God in unclear circumstances
and all of the redemptive possibilities that come from obeying
God. King understood that God drew his servants, through
circumstances, into positions of suffering to work out spiritual
issues in the person and in the community he serves. God's priority
is to temper the life of that individual as a visual example of fearless

obedience so that blessings and deliverance may be brought to a community of believers. God's purpose is always to reveal himself in love, in demonstrated power to bring glory out of gore.

King said, "every time I look at the cross I am reminded of the greatness of God and the redemptive power of Jesus Christ. I am reminded of the beauty of sacrificial love and the majesty of unswerving devotion to truth."[61] it was King's ability to see the intrinsic value of tension between opposites that enabled him to suffer debasement from his detractors, harassment from his government, and long separations from his wife and children to ensure that his life remained a channel through which God could bring freedom and social justice to blacks who had lived without it for so long in America. Fighting for full and equal justice for all in America was a new chapter in its evolution as a nation, and King was content, but not without anxiety in his willingness to suffer for the future good of America. David J. Garrow writes,

> Soon after the success of the Montgomery Bus Boycott, an organizational meeting was taking place to form the southern Christian Leadership Conference. As King began to lead the prayer at Bethel Baptist Church, he became extremely emotional. speaking to God, and with an emotional crowd responding, King spoke of the violent dangers the protesters still faced, saying, 'if anyone should be killed, let it be me.'"[62]

"Father, it is not my will, but thine be done," said Christ as he entered willingly into the determinations of God with the knowledge that his sacrifice to free the nation of Israel from religious and spiritual slavery as well as from the ideas and ruling strategies of Roman oppression, would cost him his life. King also made his own "laying down my life" utterances to God to express his self-sacrifice to what he knew lay ahead of him and of what he realized was required of a true leader inclined to go all the way with God. He wanted to carry out his purpose to bring deliverance to a population in centuries of captivity to social cruelty and domination.

If the ultimate sacrifice had to be made, King refused to deny the scepter of the bitter dregs of death for the greater cause of the movement "no one has greater love than this, to lay down one's life for one's friends."[63] some historians have suggested that King's emotional state during this prayer meeting incident at Bethel Baptist Church was the result of sheer exhaustion and depression and said, "The renewed factionalism, the bombs, and the absence of racial reconciliation depressed him. The constant travel exhausted him.[64] Depression and exhaustion may well have exacted its toll on King, but King's honest emotions cannot be discounted, downplayed, or devalued merely as a sign of exhaustion and depression, though for the nature and volume of his work and travels, he was due to be so if he were tired and depressed. The danger to his life and to those of his followers was a real and present danger. Even his wife and children were not safe from threats of violence. King did not know the day nor the hour of death's arrival—he only knew that for him, it was a certainty; and that it was only a matter of time. The threat of death was quite a burdensome mantle to carry; yet, he journeyed on through the wilderness of American hate and racial savagery—a demonstration not of weakness and confusion, but rather of strength by a spiritual leader seeking guidance from the one who called him. "You did not choose me, but I chose you and appointed you that should go and bear fruit..." (John 15:16a ESV).

Richard Lischer, in his work *The Preacher King* says:

> Early on, when King began casting himself in a prophetic role, he alluded to the necessity of suffering. In his 1958 pronouncement on prophesy he anticipates the final role of the prophet [:] 'But someone must be prepared for the ordeals of this high calling and be willing to suffer courageously for righteousness.' he would later characterize "the calling to speak" as a "vocation of agony." What appears in his early comments as a few thinly veiled hints of the dangers he and all prophets faced erupts at the end as a frank association of his own suffering with that of God's suffering servant, Jesus.[65]

In the Hebrew tradition there are two general definitions given for the term prophet. In Hebrew, the term Nabi is prophet, it derives from the verb Nabu which means to announce, call, or a declarer—to pour forth the declarations of God. God speaks through the prophet. "And whether they listen or fail to listen, for they are a rebellious house, they will know that a prophet has been among them" (Ezekiel 2:5). "And how can they hear without someone preaching to them? And how can they preach unless they are sent? As it is written, how beautiful are the feet of those who bring good news!" (Hebrews 10:14, 15). The other term used to express a prophetic call was the term Ro'eh or Ho'zeh which means "seer" and generally refers to one who predicts or foretells future events or happenings.[66] Under either definition, Martin Luther King, Jr. fit squarely into the role of prophet, and he correctly identified the call upon his life as that of prophet.

In *King's Letter from the Birmingham Jail,* we observe King as the "declarer prophet" when he challenged the apathy and indifference of the Christian church to the plight of blacks in the south. He said:

> There was a time when the church was very powerful. It was during the period when early Christians rejoiced when they were deemed worthy to suffer for what they believed. Of course King, as the "declarer prophet," often raised issues that were for the most part too hazardous for most preachers to entertain. He asked, 'is organized religion too inextricably bound to the status quo to save our nation and the world?' Maybe I must turn my faith to the inner spiritual church, the church within the church, as the true ecclesia and the hope of the world.[67]

In reference to King as prophet, Lischer writes:

> Whether a central or a peripheral figure, the prophet's most important audience is not the church but the nation, before whom he will speak words of judgment. He must steel himself with courage and be anointed with the willingness to suffer for truth.[68]

In the words of Dr. Samuel Proctor, "We need prophets to proclaim the Word of the lord, now, in the present crisis, to undo this awful state of affairs."[69] In a time of great need and urgency, Dr. King, without reluctance, stepped up and filled that prophetic void with his voice ringing out truth in a time when the country dreaded the change heeding truth must bring—resisted it violently, but it was an acceptable time for King to speak the truth.

Walter Brueggemann in his exegesis of Isaiah 47:6—11, offers a succinct summary of prophetic imagination, and proclamation concerning ambitious world power. He explains how God held a provisional alliance with the ungodly nation of Babylon under the reign of King Nebuchadnezzar as a way of chastising Israel for her disobedience.[70] No one worldwide since King has risen to prominence with the world vision and imagination of the biblical prophet. What have arisen are the myriad voices that wittingly or unwittingly, knowingly or unknowingly cast aspersions on the Gospel. These voices clamor, seek power and wealth, and make a mockery of the role of redemptive suffering as moral authority in a world that is often in desperate need of clear headed moral and spiritual leadership.

One such example nearly derailed the presidential bid of Barack Obama. Jeremiah Wright sought to link the events of 9/11 to perceived international failures due to American foreign policy decisions. He declared that God had "damned" America. Such a publically perceived, incendiary remark caused the very cynical to vicariously attribute this attitude and volatile outlook also to candidate Barack Obama—in other words, guilt by association.

In a September 13, 2001 interview, Reverend Jerry Falwell, in a telecast of the 700 Club with Reverend Pat Robertson, stated that the terrorist attacks were in part due to America turning her back on God. He said:

> And, I know that I'll hear from them for this. But, throwing God out successfully with the help of the federal courts system, throwing God out of the public square, out of the

schools[:] The abortionists have got to bear some burden for this because God will not be mocked. And when we destroy 40 million little innocent babies, we make God mad. I really believe that the pagans, the abortionists, and the feminists, and the gays and the lesbians who are actively trying to make that an alternative lifestyle, the ACLU, People For the American Way—all of them who have tried to secularize America—I point the finger in their face and say you helped this happen.[71]

Reverend Falwell, when asked about his comments, attempted to put his statement into theological terms, and said:

[I do] not believe God had anything to do with the tragedy, but that God had permitted it. He lifted the curtain of protection." he said more: "and I believe that if America does not repent and return to a genuine faith and dependence on him [God], we may expect more tragedies, unfortunately.[72]

It appears at least on those two occasions that Falwell and Wright were men who spoke for God without his counsel. The angst ridden preachers of today often fashion themselves as men of God with moral authority and concern themselves primarily with a mixture of dogmatic religious ideology, politics, and secularism. Though they'd never admit it, many of them have a craven pursuit of wealth on the backs of their unblinking followers. In the tradition of God's prophets, utterances were spoken in submission to him. In the traditional political sense, King did not jump into the fray of the body politic. His only and ultimate agenda was crystal clear: first class citizenship for blacks, and he was savvy enough to access the channels of power that he knew could help him deliver his social and economic objectives. His trajectory was totally spiritual, and not at all to seize personal power or economic gratification. Though, many attempts have been made to compare Wright's criticism of America, to King's criticism of the Vietnam War, there is a remarkable difference. if King was perceived by the establishment, both political and religious, to be stepping out of his authority, it must be remembered that King's critique of the war came many years after he had already been on the national stage. By then, he had received the Nobel Prize for Peace, and he felt that he had an obligation to speak up against a war that history has proved to be indefensible. In speaking about the Vietnam War, King said:

> Another burden of responsibility was placed upon me in 1964; and I cannot forget that the Nobel Peace Prize was also a commission, a commission to work harder than I had ever worked before for the brotherhood of man. This is a calling that takes me beyond national allegiances.[73]

Because King had established his moral leadership both nationally and internationally, his voice was not only accepted, but expected. No one questioned his stature or his motive as he appropriated his stand against the war. His prophetic role was handled with studied humility and King felt that, "a person who constantly calls attention to his trials and sufferings is in danger of developing a martyr complex and impressing others he is consciously seeking sympathy. It is impossible for one to be self-centered in his self-sacrifice."[74] So, he took himself out of the way, and from his humility could flow the oil of reconciliation and the balm of healing. His posture gave everyone who heard King the feeling that though things were tough—still, there was hope. Little of the same kind of humility and self-sacrifice are evident in self-appointed moral or spiritual leaders today. Many are openly smug provocateurs of hate and division. As Michael Dyson writes, "Whether he meant to or not, King implied that his credentials as a prophet came straight from headquarters [heaven]. Without such prophetic confidence, any seer is lost from the start."[75] Because of the seamless clarity of King's moral voice there was not much credible protestation of him regarding his sincerity, moral persuasion as he effectively blended the demands of Christian ministry with the social concerns of his day.

A 2002 Pew Foundation study found when asked how Americans felt about religion and their political leaders, they "found that while people want their leaders to be religious—they don't want them to talk about it."[76] it is possible that had such a survey been taken during King's day, many in that survey might have said, "be religious, but don't talk about it." Prophetic calls to ministry are not so simple. The position demands the one called speak out and with uncompromising clarity the truth that lands like flesh hooks on the ears of the hearers. Though King's message was widely disseminated, highly regarded, it was not always universally accepted. Nevertheless, he spoke out against the moral arbitrariness of racism and segregation—that great tragedy of his day. And in so doing, he never ceded his spiritual integrity or Christian voice to the will of man.

Also, Martin Luther King, Jr., as "seer prophet," could not relinquish his calling because what he had to say held generational significance and reckonings as does the voice of every prophet who ever lived and labored with the burden of his message and call. King saw the possibilities of the world renewed, and that the future could be different for his children, and perhaps their children. The "I have a Dream" speech captures this idea vividly and convincingly.

> And so even though we face the difficulties of today and tomorrow, I still have a dream. It is a dream deeply rooted in the American dream. I have a dream that one day this nation will rise up and live out the true meaning of its creed: "We hold these truths to be self-evident, that all men are created equal. I have a dream that one day on the red hills of Georgia, the sons of former slaves and the sons of former slave owners will be able to sit down together at the table of brotherhood. I have a dream that one day even the state of Mississippi, a state sweltering with the heat of injustice, sweltering with the heat of oppression, will be transformed into an oasis of freedom and justice.
>
> I have a dream that my four little children will one day live in a nation where they will not be judged by the color of their

skin but by the content of their character. I have a dream today! I have a dream that one day, down in Alabama, with its vicious racists, with its governor having his lips dripping with the words of "interposition" and "nullification"—one day right there in Alabama little black boys and black girls will be able to join hands with little white boys and white girls as sisters and brothers.[77]

On April 3, 1968 in Memphis, Tennessee, King elevated his "seer prophetic" status to a deeper, forceful, much more mystical place in his last sermon entitled, *I See the Promise Land*. He delivered this apocalyptic, eschatological [a haunting but prophetic end time] message, at the Mason Temple Church of God in Christ on the eve of his assassination. It was his own end time prophecy, and in his usual rhetorical splendor and oratorical flare, he said:

We've got some difficult days ahead. But it doesn't matter with me now. Because I've been to the mountain top. And I don't mind. Like anybody, I would like to live a long life. Longevity has its place. But I'm not concerned about that now. I just want to do God's will. And he's allowed me to go up to the mountain. And I've looked over. And I've seen the Promised Land. I may not get there with you. But I want you to know tonight, that we, as a people will get to the Promised Land. And I'm happy, tonight. I'm not worried about anything. I'm not fearing any man. Mine eyes have seen the glory of the coming of the lord.[78]

Earlier in his work, King recalled that one night, being fearful and frustrated, unable to sleep; he went into the kitchen to have a cup of coffee, and while there he began to pray. He recalled, "it seemed as though I could hear the quiet assurance of an inner voice saying: 'Martin Luther, stand up for righteousness. Stand up for justice. Stand up for truth. And lo, I will be with you. Even until the end of the world.'"[79]

Like the Old Testament prophet Samuel, Martin Luther King, Jr., having been conscious of his divine call (I Samuel 3:15—20), having reluctantly accepted the mantle to lead the Montgomery Bus Boycott, had come to the end of his work and journey here on earth. King's fears and his determination to walk into them without wavering, had transformed the nation. His faith in God lifted this nation, and enabled it to give new birth to itself; to accept its formidable founding principles as viable and applicable to everyone in the country. By standing for righteousness, justice and truth, King had affirmed the traditional Christian belief in the redemptive power of suffering. In so doing, he elevated the concept of suffering and its symbolism with undiluted truth.[80] he saw the symbolic truth of the cross in its definitive redemptive power, he said:

> As I behold the uplifted cross I am reminded not only of the unlimited power of God, but also of the sordid weakness of man. I think not only of the radiance of the divine, but also the tang of the human. I am reminded not only of Christ at his best, but man at his worst[81]

Stanley Hauerwas said, "Jesus' cross, however, is not merely a general symbol of the moral significance of self-sacrifice. Rather the cross is Jesus' ultimate dispossession through which God has conquered the powers of this world.[82] as King himself said, "not every minister can be a prophet, but some must be prepared for the ordeals of this high calling and be willing to suffer courageously for righteousness."[83] Dr. King urged the black community not to succumb to the negativity and pessimism that currently surrounded the Civil Rights Movement, but to take those events and turn them into something "creative and redeeming."

Lewis Baldwin framed this feeling in terms of imbedded Christian optimism in African American cultural heritage. "King and his people in the south, like their slave fore parents, subscribed unquestionably to the providential view that God controls history and the universe, and that God's plan for all humanity would ultimately be fulfilled."[84] Dr. King saw suffering as a transformative experience that if responded to rightly could be profoundly useful. He expressed as much in saying:

My personal trials have also taught me the value of unmerited suffering. As my sufferings mounted I soon realized that there were two ways that I could respond to my situation: either to react with bitterness or seek to transform the suffering into a creative force. I decided to follow the latter course. Recognizing the necessity for suffering I have tried to make of it a virtue.[85]

This idea of a suffering servant provided the faith necessary to overcome mob beatings, death threats, and jailing, and even death.

King echoed this theology when he eulogized the four little girls who were killed in the sixteenth street Baptist Church bombing on September 15, 1963. "So they did not die in vain. God still has a way of wringing good out of evil. History has proven over and over again that unmerited suffering is redemptive."[86] even in this horrific event, King is moved to believe that suffering is a natural means of achieving ultimate freedom and social justice. Not unlike the words expressed by the German Philosopher Hegel, who "understands that to have value in my own eyes I must achieve value in the eyes of others.[87] According to King:

The way of nonviolence means a willingness to suffer and sacrifice. It may mean going to jail if such is the case. The resistor must be willing to fill the jailhouses of the south. It may even mean physical death. But if physical death is the price that a man must pay to free his children and his white brethren from a permanent death of the spirit, then nothing more could be more redemptive.[88]

King's willingness to suffer as a means of bringing forth a redemptive purpose reveals his highly developed cognition, his high degree of moral reasoning. The moral educator, Lawrence Kohlberg's innovative way of observing stages of moral reasoning categorizes seven stages of cognitive development. In the Kohlberg theory each stage represents a higher development of cognitive moral reasoning ability. The seventh stage is considered the highest and most developed stage of moral reasoning. Kohlberg identifies Martin Luther King, Jr., as one of his "moral exemplars." Those who are willing to give their life for what they believe. in a religious context, Kohlberg, identifies, King as "profoundly religious, willing to die for [his] principles, which are partly based on [his] faith in reason and partly on [his] faith in justice, which has a religious support."[89] King understood that to follow Jesus Christ and to aspire for the excellence of God's Kingdom were the supreme "exemplars" to which each follower must strive to conform. Michael Gorman characterizes this as "Cruciformity," which means to identify with Christ and his cross in a redemptive context (Galatians 2:20, 21; Philippians 3:10). "For Paul, the experience of dying with Christ, though intensely personal, can never be private. Fundamentally, Cruciformity means community, and community means cruciformity."[90] and King said,

> As Christian, we must never surrender our supreme loyalty to any time-bound custom or earth-bound idea, for at the heart of our universe is a higher reality—God and his kingdom of love—to which we must be conformed. This command to conform comes, not only from Paul, but also from our lord and Master, Jesus Christ, the world's most dedicated nonconformist, whose ethical nonconformity still challenges the conscience of mankind.[91]

On September 17, 1958, King was conducting a book signing in a most unusual setting, the shoe section of Blumstein's department store in Harlem.[92] While autographing his newly released book *Stride toward Freedom*, a woman, obviously deranged, identified as Ms. Izola Ware Curry, drew a seven inch letter opener from inside her coat and thrust it into Dr. King's neck. It grazed his aorta and narrowly spared his life[93] King, who acted with Christ-like forgiveness, forgave his attacker. Later, in reference to that experience he said:

If I demonstrated unusual calm during the recent attempt on my life it was certainly not due to any extraordinary powers that I possess. Rather, it was due to the power of God working through me. Throughout this struggle for racial justice I have constantly asked God to remove all bitterness from my heart and to give me the strength and courage to face any disaster that came my way."[94] Just as the criminals who crucified Jesus, he said, 'Father forgive them; for they do not what they are doing.' (Luke 23:34). Amazingly, after a successful surgery that required the removal of two ribs and a portion of his breast bone, one of the doctors told King, if he merely sneezed he could have punctured the aorta and would have died almost immediately from massive internal bleeding.[95] Though King recovered from the tragic attack, only a prophet who followed the precepts and teaching of Christ would ultimately be left with a scar, a scar in the shape of a cross, right over his heart.[96]

The turbulence that surrounded King's activism did not distract him. He kept his focus on his relationship with God, on service to his community and he continued to confront his country. He felt America had not yet lived up to its potential to all its citizens. King's voice remained compelling and empathetic. It echoed the concerns of life's deepest contradictions against his constituency. It mounted convincing arguments on the highest moral grounds; and—yet, his voice and message was entirely accessible to the day-to-day needs and everyday concerns of his listeners.

CHAPTER SIX

Martin Luther King Jr. and the Global Age: Implications for International Peace and Social Justice

———— ✳ ————

"He is a God who opposes evil and injustice and oppression. He is a God who sides with those who are oppressed because He's that kind of God, and not because the oppressed are morally better than their oppressors".[97] Bishop Tutu

WHILE IT IS TRUE that the life works of Martin Luther King, Jr. was rooted in the African American struggle for justice and human equality in America, his activities had a global reach that has not been as much heralded as his work at home. Of course, the issues he addressed, peace, nonviolence, human rights, economic inequality, freedom of religious expression, adequate food and shelter, and justice for all people reached into the struggles and concerns of nation states and like-minded individuals around the world. And it is fair to say that King's opposition to the War in Vietnam was the beginning of his international approach to advocating for human rights.

On March 4, 1957, King visited Ghana in West Africa. The invitation was extended to him along with a large number of American political leaders, including then Vice-President, Richard Nixon, and civil rights leaders, by the newly elected president Kwame Nkrumah. Dignitaries from around the world attended the ceremony to mark the independence of Ghana as "the first independent nation of sub-Saharan Africa".[98] King said, "The minute I knew I was coming to Ghana I had a very deep emotional feeling. A new nation was being born. It symbolized the fact that a new order was coming into being and an old order was passing away."[99] King, when telling his congregation about his experience in Ghana elaborated and said:

> A handsome black man walked out on the platform, and he was followed by eight or ten other men. He stood there and said, "We are no longer a British colony. We are a free and sovereign people." When he uttered those words, we looked back and saw an old flag coming down and a new flag going up. And I said to myself, That old flag coming down doesn't represent the meaning of this drama taking place on the stage of history, for it is the symbol of an old order passing away. That new flag going up is a symbol of a new age coming into being. I could hear people shouting all over that vast audience, Freedom! Freedom! Before I knew it, I started weeping. I was crying for joy. And I knew about all of the struggles, all of the pain, and all of the agony that these people had gone through for this moment.[100]

King's trip to Ghana opened an affinity he would thereafter have for Africa and its people: "American blacks could learn some important lessons from the freedom struggles that Africans have waged against European colonialists, he said"[101] Though as moved and happy as he was about what was happening in Ghana, there was the stark contrast of what was happening in South Africa, which practiced a particularly brutal form of apartheid. Implemented in 1948, it would last until 1990.

On December 10, 1965, Human Rights Day at Hunter College, New York City, Dr. King demonstrated his commitment to fighting injustice globally. In a speech that day he made a passionate and poignant indictment against the government of South Africa. The speech also provided a glimpse into the prophetic mind of King. The speech included three themes that would foreshadow the ultimate demise of the apartheid system of government in South Africa. The first theme King addressed was the ill-conceived notion which had persisted well into the 20th century that blacks are genetically inferior to their white counterparts. King said "Africa has been depicted for more than a century as the home of black cannibals and ignorant primitives. Despite volumes of facts contraverting this picture, the stereotypes persist in books, motion pictures, and other media of communication."[102] in Basil Moore's work, *The Challenge of Black Theology in South Africa*, he suggests that the Christian Church in South Africa is complicit in its perpetuation of negative propagandizing of black Africa, Moore writes:

> In South Africa the Christian Church has probably been one of the most powerful instruments in making possible the political oppression of the black people. While the white colonists were busy with the process of robbing the people of their land and their independence, the Churches were busy, however unconsciously, undermining the will of the people to resist. This was done in a number of subtle and not so subtle ways. In the first place the Church made it plain that everything African was heathen and superstitious barbarism. Conversion to Christianity meant rejecting traditional forms of dress, authority, social organization, culture, marriage, medicine, etc. The black people were made to believe not that salvation is in Christ alone, but that salvation is in accepting the new white ways of living. The effect of this was to internalize in the black people a sense of the inferiority which inhered in them as Africans.[103]

In Edwin M. Yamauchi's work, *Africa and the Bible*, Yamauchi provides the historical context for the rise of apartheid involving one the most devastating theories related to the myth of the inferiority of African peoples which began in South Africa but spread to North America in the late nineteenth century. He writes:

> Between 1836 and 1846, ten thousand descendants of Dutch colonists called Boers of Afrikaners escaped British jurisdiction to the Cape Colony by trekking into the interior of South Africa. There they defeated the Zulus in the battle of Blood River in 1838 and subjugated various tribes, such as the Khoikhoi and the Hottentots. According to George Fredrickson, the Trekboers invoked the curse of ham to justify expansion.[104]

In the context of American slave history, Dr. Anthony Evans says, "the church became another major contributor to the expansion of both sides of the myth. Hiding behind a hermeneutic based on cultural expedience rather than exegetical integrity; the White church endorsed the societally accepted status of itself as superior and Blacks as inferior.[105] In fact, Evans explains the ridiculous nature of the Hamitic curse assertion:

> Never mind, of course, that the Bible says that Canaan was cursed, not Ham. Thus, only one of Ham's four sons, not all four, was cursed. Therefore, all Black people everywhere could not be cursed. Never mind that the Bible placed limitations on curses for up to three or four generations (Exodus 20:5). Never mind that the curse on Canaan and his descendants finds its most obvious fulfillment in the ongoing defeat and subjugation of Canaan by Israel (Joshua 9:23; I Kings 9:20, 21). Never mind that the other sons of ham have continued to this day as national people in Cush (Ethiopia), Mizraim (Egypt), and Pt (Libya). On the other hand, Canaan is the only son that has not continued to exist as a nation. Most important of all, curses based on disobedience are reversed when there is repentance and obedience (Exodus 20:6), which is certainly sufficient to negate the Christian endorsement of American enslavement of Black Christians.[106]

Evan's says, and rightly so, that "the perpetuation of the inferiority myth is as much psychological as it is theological, because myths affect the way people think."[107] King's childhood experience of growing up in the segregated south no doubt affected him greatly; particularly, when he talked about how black parents might explain the circumstances of the divided world in which they lived. of his own mother, he says, "she tried to explain the divided system of the south—segregated schools, restaurants, theaters, housing; the white and colored signs on drinking fountains, waiting rooms, lavatories—as a social condition rather than a natural order. Then she said the words that almost every Negro hears before he can yet understand the injustice that make them necessary: "You are as good as anyone."[108] As echoed in King's speech at Hunter College, he expressed his disdain for the notion of white superiority when he said, "The South African Government to make the white supreme has had to reach into the past and revive the nightmarish ideology and practices of Nazism."[109] King often remarked: "a doctrine of black supremacy is as evil as a doctrine of white supremacy.[110]

Thusly, the second theme King addressed in his speech was a comparison of the horrors of the slave trade, and the South African system of apartheid to that of the Jewish Holocaust, saying:

> There are few parallels in human history of the period in which Africans were seized and branded like animals, packed into ships' holds like cargo and transported into chattel slavery. Millions suffered agonizing death in the middle passage in a holocaust reminiscent of the Nazi slaughter of Jews and Poles, and others."[111]

It was not a mere coincidence that King so readily and so sensitively associated the struggles of African Americans with struggles of Jewish people during Hitler's rule in Nazi Germany. In 1963, Dr. King developed a unique bond; a soul like friendship with Rabbi Abraham Joshua Heschel, an orthodox Jew of Warsaw and descendant from dynastic generations of Hasidic Rabbis.[112] Both men were attending a Chicago Conference on Religion and Race. "The two men were drawn to each other by a shared commitment to the language and experience of the Hebrew prophets."[113] During Heschel's conference presentation, he said, "The exodus began, but is far from having been completed. In fact, it was easier for the children of Israel to cross the Red sea than for a Negro to cross certain university campuses."[114] No doubt, referring to similar experiences, such as what took place when James Meredith had literally to be escorted by us Marshalls in order to attend classes at university of Mississippi.[115] Two years after the Chicago Conference, Rabbi Heschel joined King, walking side by side with him in the Selma to Montgomery march. "Heschel declared later: 'When I marched in Selma, my feet were praying.'"[116] During the Civil years of 50's and 60's there was a strong Jewish-Black alliance that was linked by a common struggle for justice.

The third theme King addressed in his speech at Hunter College was his charge of human rights violations and economic exploitation of the majority population without reprisal. King, said "South Africa says to the world: 'We have become a powerful industrial economy; we are too strong to be defeated by paper resolution of world tribunals; we are immune to protest and economic reprisals.'"[117]

The speech highlighted King's breadth of knowledge of the plight of South Africans, and exemplified his concerns for their supplications for equality. Before the 1980's legislation of the Sullivan Plan to Divest in South Africa, King, in 1962, had already asked people to hold meetings and demonstrations to encourage world governments to support economic sanctions against South Africa. On December 10, he implored, "Write to your mission at the united nations urging adoption of a resolution calling for international isolation of South Africa; don't buy South African products; don't trade or invest in South Africa.".[118]

Remarkably, King sought to deploy the forces of the global market economy to dislodge the cruel forces of oppression in South Africa. If economic boycotts could work in America to alleviate oppression for blacks, it might also work to do the same for the oppressed blacks of South Africa. He said:

The misery of the poor in Africa and Asia is shared misery, a fact of life for the vast majority; they are all poor together as a result of years of exploitation and underdevelopment.[119] Our missionary efforts fail when they are based on pity, rather than true compassion. Instead of seeking to do something with the African and Asian people, we have too often sought only to do something for them.[120]

The precision with which King makes his arguments identifies what is usually the root cause of oppression in the first place: money! King criticized America for its investments in the motor and rubber industries in South Africa. He was critical of South Africa's gold mining industry and its exploitive use of black Africans to extract this precious metal from the earth. King pointed to the fact that millions were being spent by America in South Africa to assist with technical support in building nuclear reactors, an action which further re-enforced South Africa's dominance over oppressed black Africans.

King's anti-apartheid crusade against South African atrocities against its citizens was just as impassioned as his anti-segregation crusade against the vileness of racial injustice in America. It was a biblical call to justice for all people beyond the boundaries of his own country. He recognized the systemic ability of men to be cruel to other men: an age old problem whose call makes King's prophetic voice not unlike the prophetic call of the eighth century prophet Amos. Amos also condemned the people of Israel for the corrupt legal systems that oppressed the poor. The prophet declared:

> Therefore because you trample on the poor and take from them levies of grain, you have built houses of hewn stone, but you have not lived in them; you have planted pleasant vineyards, but you shall not drink their wine. For I know how many are your transgressions, and how great are your sins—you who afflict the righteous, who take a bribe, and push aside the needy in the gate (Amos 5:11—12).

Like a true member of the body of Christ, King hurt for American blacks and he hurt for Africa's blacks. To raise his voice against South African oppression was a call to solidarity and compassion for not only South Africans, but for the oppressed anywhere on the globe.

It took great courage for King to speak out on injustice on the international stage, but he did it. And subsequent to his trip to West Africa, King visited India. Through a grant from The American Friends service Committee, the Christopher Reynolds Foundation, and the Quaker organization, King visited the country accompanied by his wife, Coretta Scott King and his friend Professor Lawrence Reddick of Alabama State College, in February 1959. Both men were interested in the education programs in the Gandhian Nonviolence Centers. Reddick also had written a King biography entitled: *Crusader Without Violence.* King spent a month in India meeting with government leaders and activist in the Gandhian movement. During this visit, Mrs. Coretta King examined the role of women in the Indian Independence Movement."[121] King remarked "the Indian people loved to listen to the Negro spirituals. Therefore, Coretta ended up singing as much as I lectured."[122]

The influence of Mahatma Gandhi and his peaceful non-violent struggles for Indian liberation upon King's ministry is well documented; King's night of silence spent in the bedroom that was once Gandhi's to imbibe his quietness and peaceful ethos. Apart from the application of Gandhi's strategies, King's interest in Gandhi's methods illustrated his understanding of the interconnectedness of the human struggle for liberty—that human liberty is not simply and ideal, it is a mandate of the human spirit laid there by God. The essential truth that provided King's prophetic struggles with momentum and formation and direction is the truth that all men and women want to be free. King's unique ability to see the common global connections between people around the world who had shared experiences of suffering, disenfranchisements and injustice, informed the global thrust of his advocacy

Also, in 1959, King developed plans to expand his global peace initiatives with a trip to Russia.

> He planned to spend several weeks consulting with Christian leaders in the Soviet Union following his stay in India. Money for the trip to Russia was donated by the American Baptist Convention. The American Baptist Convention passed a resolution in 1956 calling for the establishment of Christian fellowship across international boundaries as a step toward understanding and peace.[123]

In the end, King did not make the trip to Russia. The urgency of conditions in the south at the time forestalled the trip. His desire to do so further demonstrated his global vision and the scope of his concern for peace worldwide.

In 1967, King planned to visit Israel on an ecumenical pilgrimage. King's assistant Andrew Young who worked with the Israeli foreign ministry arranged for King "to preach to as many as five thousand travelers from a boat just offshore on the sea of Galilee."[124] Those plans were derailed by war and King postponed his trip to the region. "Riots over operation shredder, a quick predawn raid on Palestinian militia near Hebron turned into a pitched battle with the unexpected arrival of a Jordanian army patrol. It was a significant and bloody incursion. The Israeli commander of the operation and fifteen Jordanian legionnaires were killed...."[125] in the same year, June 1967, the six-Day War between Israel and the neighboring states of Egypt, Jordan, and Syria took place. "Taylor Branch writes:

> Instantly, by contrast, the outbreak of the Middle East War threw the Vietnam Peace Movement into a political crossfire. Martin Luther King, back from Geneva, smarted from criticism that he had abandoned non-violence by lending his name with Reinhold Niebuhr and other religious leaders to a prewar *New York Times* ad that sounded alarm over hostile Arab encirclement."[126]

King's international travel and human rights involvement brought into clear vision his concept of the "beloved community" or the "world house" which was his vision of the growing intersections of a world shrinking daily. King foresaw and understood how the world economy would become so increasingly intertwined that his concern for the poor of America also translated into concern for the poor of Africa, Asia and the disenfranchised of every third world nation around the globe. After he received the Nobel Peace Prize, King said "I now had to give a great deal of attention to the three problems which I considered as the largest of those that confront mankind: racial injustice around the world, poverty, and war. Though each appeared to be separate and isolated, all were interwoven into a single garment of man's destiny."[127]

Thomas l. Friedman, columnist for the *New York Times* defines this interconnectedness in this way:

> The inexorable integration of markets, nation-states and technologies to a degree never witnessed before—in a way that is enabling individuals, corporations and nation-states to reach around the world farther, faster deeper, cheaper than ever before"[128]

Yet long before Friedman conceptualize globalization, King profoundly and eloquently said, "We are all caught in an inescapable network of mutuality, tied into a single garment of destiny. Whatever affects one directly, affects all indirectly. We are made to live together because of the interrelated structure of reality."[129] In King's view, plenty for one should mean enough for "the least of these" regardless of national or international boundaries; the world community should together seek global peace and social economic justice. He said:

> This is a great new problem of mankind. We have inherited a large house, a great 'world house in which we have to live together—black and white, easterner and Westerner, Gentile and Jew, Catholic and Protestant, Moslem and Hindu—a

family unduly separated in ideas, culture and interest, who, because we can never again live apart, must learn somehow to live with each other in peace.[130]

Today the global problems are much more complex. Issues of peace and poverty are just two of the many other issues facing international communities. Issues from the sustainability of the environment, terrorism, human trafficking, drug trafficking have also become major challenges for those working on behalf of world justice. In fact, the U.S. Department of Health and Human Services contends human trafficking is a form of modern-day slavery, "widespread throughout the united states today. Trafficking of humans is the second largest criminal industry in the world after drug dealing."[131] According to U.S. Department of health and human services fact sheet:

> Approximately 600,000 to 800,000 victims annually are trafficked across international borders worldwide, according to the U.S. Department of State. These estimates include women, men and children. Victims are generally trafficked into the U.S. from Asia, Central and South America, and Eastern Europe. Many victims trafficked into the United States do not speak and understand English and are therefore isolated and unable to communicate with service providers, law enforcement and others who might be able to help them.[132]

Certainly, King would fine these blighted human conditions to be right causes of his advocacy. In *The Measure of a Man*, he writes "The breadth of life is that dimension of life in which we are concerned about others. An individual has not started living until [he/she] can rise above the narrow confines of his individualistic concerns to the broader concerns of all humanity."[133] King wrote these words after telling the story of the "Good Samaritan" found in Luke 10:29—37. The central question for him was: who is my neighbor? The story portrays a man who traveled from Jerusalem to Jericho and along the way was robbed, beaten, abused by thieves. They left him on the side of the road half dead. A priest and Levite saw him but both passed him by without rendering aid.

But a *Good* Samaritan who saw him stopped and ministered to his needs and demonstrated a humane and neighborly response.

The global connectivity of the ideology of Martin Luther, King Jr., could not have been more apparent than in 2007 when the Chinese Government permitted a theatrical play about Martin Luther King to be presented in Beijing. The drama was performed in Chinese with a Chinese actor cast in the role of King. The play's director, Wu Xiaojiang said, "as China makes gradual progress in politics, I think people will get a clearer understanding of this play's message. They won't reject it because they think it differs from China's ideology. We may even find things worth borrowing for our own social advancement."[134] The impact of Martin Luther King's global reach is yet fully to be known, however there is no doubt his vision, voice and message continues to expand the globe.

CHAPTER SEVEN

I Know I've been changed: Reconciliation and Social Reform

❋

"We pray here that heaven may be duplicated on earth through the moral and spiritual transformation of humanity, both in its personal units and its corporate life."[135] *Walter Rauschenbusch*

FOR CENTURIES MANY BLACKS made their churches a place of refuge from a hostile society. The church was the place where the creative and service potentials of each member could be tapped and utilized in harmony with the needs of the entire membership to move the local agenda of a congregation forward. In the black community, there was no discernable culture of black church fragmentation or dislocation. Generations of families joined a church, stayed there, and made a difference—good or bad. Such a tradition of membership cohesion and longevity formed long bonds of friendship and provided people with a sense of belonging in a smaller group since there were no natural or common niches for them in the larger society.

For a season, this was the reservoir of energy and spiritual power, sheer grit and determination, into which Dr. King tapped to deliver his message of human dignity and equality. Under his leadership, the characteristic of the black church went from safe haven to social laboratory in the wake of the 1955 Rosa Parks incident. Appreciated for centuries for the lively spirituals, gospel music, and colorful preaching, it is this very atmosphere that had tempered and slowly seasoned King for life's rugged struggle in a society not yet convinced of its moral responsibility for social justice and reform.

God's time for America and the role of the Black Church had come—too, for the greater white church had it been willing and obedient. According to Robert Scofield, King thought:

> The purpose of the church was not to create dogma, theology, or creeds but rather 'to produce living witnesses and testimonies to the power of God in human experience.'... King viewed the church's role as promoting a way of life rather than a belief system, saying, 'Jesus always recognized that there is a danger of having a high blood pressure of creeds and an anemia of deeds...that Christ is more concerned with how we treat our neighbors, our attitudes toward social justice, and living a high ethical life than he is with long processionals, knowledge of creeds, or the beautiful architecture of a church.'[136]

For more than two and a half centuries, the cries and prayers of oppressed blacks had come up to before the throne of God waiting there, according to acts 10:4, as a memorial before him. God's timing and King's pinpoint seizure of the moment with Rosa Parks and the Montgomery Bus Boycott launched the larger forum of the Civil Rights Movement and the Black Church into its most significant social, spiritual and political purpose since the rise of the independent Black Church Movement in late 1700's led by black preachers such as Richard Allen, Absalom Jones and George Liele.

King's election for the task to lead the civil rights movement was not solely of the will of man, nor of King's intellectual prowess, did he have a clear vision of God's ordained destiny for him. As he stated, had he a moment to consider the magnitude of the task, he might have chosen not to take it.[137] he simply believed this was the right thing to do and he was led of the Holy Spirit into a modern day wilderness, he willingly submitted to God to go there.

The overarching picture of the Civil Rights Movement was clear example of God's ongoing desire to free man of his lower nature and to be fully reconciled to him. King wrote,

> ...every time we turn our backs to the low road and accept the high road, every time we say no to self that we may say yes to Jesus Christ, every time a man or [woman] turns from ugliness to beauty and is able to forgive their enemies...Jesus stands at the door of our hearts if we are willing to admit him...we turn our lives to the highest and [the] best there for us is the Christ.[138]

If the struggle for Civil Rights changed the country externally, God's ongoing change in Martin Luther King and the Black Church internally was the key to the movement's success. When King was called out by the lord to help set people free, it confirmed his sense of God's call. Furthermore, it was a challenge given to the country to spearhead this transformative campaign that moved the Black Church from—strength to strength—a safe house—to a mighty force with which America had finally to reckon. King's personal response to the circumstances before him was to jostle the sleeping giant awake he observed too long resting in the pews of the Black Church, he said:

> Where is that kind of fervor today? Where is that kind of daring, revolutionary commitment to Christ today? Is it hidden behind smoke screens and altars? Is it buried in a grace called respectability? Is it inextricably bound with nameless status quos and imprisoned within cells of stagnant mores?[139]

King believed that in the hands of God, the church could become the "hope of the world" as Christ intended it to be. Until the middle of the twentieth-century, America was a nation in the throes of the darkest most intractable form of demon inspired pride and severe oppression of the rights of its black citizens. Nowhere in the country was this more evident than on Bloody Sunday, March 7, 1965, when demonstrators tried to cross the Edmund Pettus Bridge from Selma to Montgomery, Alabama. They simply wanted to make an appeal on behalf of their constitutional right to "one man one vote" and to speak to Governor George Wallace about the murders of innocent marchers. Instead, they were met with summary violence and brute force from the Alabama state Police.

Theophillus Eugene "Bull" Connor, the commissioner of public safety in Birmingham, Alabama, was another powerful symbol of southern racial bigotry. His use of dogs, fire hoses and police batons against Civil Rights workers exhibited the grave conditions under which blacks lived in the state of Alabama and throughout the south. If Martin Luther King ever wanted to lay down the cross he had picked up; during these awful events was the time to do it. He, however had steadfastly, put his hand to the blood stained plow. King believed that unity with God necessarily required "moral struggle and self-renunciation." in keeping with his belief, he gathered more courage, put his shoulder to the wheel, mobilized the troops, as destiny continued to beckon him.

With a firm boot of selfishness of one race on the neck of another, everyone was captive to the lies that God had made a subhuman black race that was subservient to a far superior white race. As stated earlier, this idea was similar to the views held in the South African apartheid system, supported by the long held and erroneous theological conviction that God had cursed ham through his son Canaan with black skin and consigned him to forever serve his brother, of white skin. Such dissonant logic served as a wonderful ointment to sooth those who believed this an excuse to call what God created evil or bad—*or*, if God cursed them—we can also. The consequences of that level of staggering pride are that one part of the white race was steadfastly cold and insensitive to the plight of blacks. They felt manifestly entitled to everything America had to offer as far as the eye could see. They had no desire to or intention of sharing any of what America, the wealthiest and most productive nation in human history, had to offer. One part was too protective of what they owned to do anything about what was happening to their black neighbors. They burrowed into their familiar comforts and waited for the dust to settle; not only that, this same group poked their heads out far enough and just long enough to warn King that he was moving too fast, asking too much. Famously, in his *Letter from the Birmingham Jail*, King specifically addressed the woes of this crowd by way of their clergy. He wrote, "We know through painful experience that freedom is never voluntarily given by the oppressor; it must be demanded by the oppressed."[140] White churchmen were ominously cowardly in the face of the Civil Rights Movement. It appeared they preferred their sinful status quo to any minute effort at confronting the racists who sat in their pews each Sunday. Silent white Christians of that day helped evil to triumph. They either sat or stood idly by and did nothing in the face of great darkness. They were like fig trees in full bloom out of season—impotent in a time of need—with no faith and no works.

In a letter to the Church at Laodicea, Jesus roundly rebuked those for sitting in the seat of indifference. "I know thy works, that thou art neither cold nor hot; I would thou wert cold or hot. So then because thou art lukewarm, and neither hot nor cold, will I spew thee out of my mouth (Rev.3:15—16). Christ "gave himself for us, that he might redeem us from all iniquity, and purify unto himself a peculiar people, zealous of good works" (Titus 2:14). In that time, it was a sad testimony that too many Christians were peculiar, but not zealous of good works for the kingdom of God.

On the other hand, King was an avowed instrument of God and an agent of change who often quoted Edmund Burke who said, "all that is necessary for the triumph of evil is that good men do nothing"[141] Evil, sin and the activities of men who inspire, promote and support evil must be opposed. Left unchecked for centuries, discrimination against blacks proliferated to the degree that a black life had no legal, moral or spiritual value in the United States outside its own community. Many pious Christians, black, white and other, have not yet accepted the fact that good is not merely the absence of doing evil—the truth of goodness lies in whether good men are willing to stand up in the face of evil and do what is right. This is the truth Martin Luther King, Jr. comprehended all too well. It is another seminal reality which provided impetus for his work.

For King, justice and the pursuit of righteousness was a dynamic spiritual force that would make the difference. God would support good, and eschew evil. His liberal blending of justice, love, peace and faith evoked a powerful fusion of his message of dignity and self-worth. His singular vision and his moral authority became the conscience of a nation that did not fully understand that one can only pursue what is good and just and pure and virtuous if he is aware of and is fully convinced of his own humanity and inherent dignity. It is at this pivotal place that his voice strikes its resonance, makes it clear that the theology of hate did not come from a heart of good will and love of oneself and country.

Today, it may be credibly argued that Martin Luther King, Jr. accomplished more for the cause of human rights in America and around the world than any leader in the twentieth century. The moral force of righteousness superseded evil and complacency. King believed if more leaders of his day chose to practice, servant hood, as exemplified by Jesus Christ, the church and it congregants could, together, ascend to its highest call. Throughout the course of his life, he practiced and encouraged abandonment to the causes of God by members of the church. The other part of whites, and people of all hues in the nation, was fully willing to walk the hard walk, to lay down their lives alongside King and other blacks in the struggle for equality in America.

In his *I Have a Dream* speech Dr. King advocated for a more open society in which all Americans could participate.

When the architects of our republic wrote the magnificent words of the Constitution and the Declaration of independence, they were signing a promissory to which every American heir. This note was the promise that all men, yes, black men as well as white men, would be guaranteed the unalienable rights of life, liberty, and the pursuit of happiness.[142]

The Framers of the Constitution recognized God as the "The Creator," and the "supreme Judge of the world." They recognized that God's hand was at work in the affairs of the new nation. King recognized that his was the only major national document of the United States that actually mentions the name of God. As such, long ago, God had been invited into and included in the affairs of America. In Ecclesiastes, Solomon said that "it is God's gift that all should eat and drink and take pleasure in all their toil." (Eccl. 3:13) Blacks had been too long deprived of this God-given blessing and human right. Even though it seemed that God's plan had been averted; it was not. God's intended plan for America—its good is for all. The covenant enshrined in the Constitution of the united states with *all* the citizens of America, he would bring to pass.

Yet, one is still left to ponder, and it is certain to have been a contemplation of Martin Luther King, Jr. that a people, many of whose ancestors had fled Great Britain to escape tyranny and oppression would so soon forget the nightmarish scenario that drove them off the British shores, the cruel autocracy that encompasses oppression, denial, dehumanization and degradation of other people's lives. There stood King, nonetheless, in the sweltering late summer heat of Washington, D.C. on august 27, 1963, attempting to overcome the nightmare with his *"Dream"* reminding the nation that on July 4, 1776, at the second Continental Congress, when the delegates declared the thirteen American colonies free and independent from Great Britain, this freedom extended, in fact, to everyone in America.

CHAPTER EIGHT

Stand up for Justice: Moral Consciousness for the 21st Century

— ✻ —

"Costly grace is the gospel which must be sought again and again, the gift which must be asked for, the door at which a [person] must knock. Such grace is costly because it calls us to follow, and it is grace because it calls us to follow Jesus Christ."[26]
Bonheoffer

THE REALITIES OF HUMAN suffering and deprivation did not hamper Dr. Martin Luther King, Jr.'s high degree of idealism. Nor did it interfere with his ability to believe that there was a solution to the problems beyond what his eyes could see. Inspirational faith was a key motivational aspect of the way King approached and dealt with the immense problems of social injustice that confronted him, the problems of the people he referred to as his own. King also recognized that the problems of human oppression were not unique to black Americans. He saw the world and the country lying before him as a template of what is possible to do to help lift people from culturally and socially entrenched injustices—that what he advocated for in America to relieve people of suffering would have enormous influence on suffering people around the globe.

King once said "The oppressed must never allow the conscience of the oppressor to slumber…To accept injustice or segregation passively is to say to the oppressor that his actions are morally right."[27] Dr. King acknowledged fully that he could not stand idly by and do nothing while people suffered under social tyranny. and he clearly understood that most social problems faced by oppressed peoples were spiritual and emanated from the darkest areas of the hearts of men and women who allowed their pride unchecked to so inspire them, they felt free to take what did not belong solely to them—to assume postures of superiority to which they were not morally endowed, spiritually or rightfully entitled.

King acknowledged the power invested in the church by God to "bring the good news of the gospel" to those who had an ear to hear was his responsibility as a child of God. This number of hearers, of course, included the oppressed themselves who had to first hear the gospel of liberation and understand that they had a place, and an accepted time to stand up, to demand their God-given rights for liberty and equality. It takes no grand leap of the imagination to see eye to eye with King that the besetting nature of racism and oppression are deep-rooted spiritual problems. The roots of which sprang from the flaws left exposed in the founding principles of the country (that all men—*not just white men were created equal*). The precision of King's objections and confrontations targeted these presumptions as much from the pulpit as from the streets of protest, the church and specifically his pulpit was used as a militant agency for change and redress of what was lacking in the Constitution of the united states and succeeding laws governing human and race relations in the nation.

So often, King's critics attacked him for blending the spiritual affairs of the church with the secular matters of civil rights. They accused him of [taking actions] that moved the church beyond its accepted boundaries of shepherding the spiritual. If dislodging hate from the hearts of white Americans against black Americans was beyond the pale of spiritual shepherding; of that, King made no distinction. Instead, he proceeded with confidence in his agenda knowing that his failure to be engaged in civil rights on a spiritual plane would result in failure. For him to vacate his spiritual activities would have meant a capitulation of his core moral values, a denial and a betrayal of the foundation that formed the worldview he held so dearly. King's response to his critics that he inserted the moral and spiritual authority of the church into the role of addressing social and moral problems as follows:

> Most emphatically, the essence of the epistles of Paul is that Christians should rejoice at being deemed worthy to suffer for what they believe. The projection of a social gospel, in my opinion, is the true witness of a Christian life. This is the meaning of the true ecclesia—the inner, spiritual church. The church once changed society. It was then a thermostat of society. But today I feel that too much of the church is merely a thermometer, which measures, rather molds popular opinion...as one whose Christian roots go back through three generations of ministers—My father, grandfather, and great-grandfather—I will remain true to the church as long as I live.[28]

His was a unique mixture of evangelical liberalism and his comprehension of social justice. In addition, King's theology was one of practice: faith *with* works. King's positioning of himself in the church to respond to his critics in terms of militant agency confirmed his theological customs. Dr. Charles Adams, in his sermon *Faith Critiques Faith*, pointed out that Martin Luther King was "politically involved, but was also godly enough to maintain his theological integrity and his political independence."[29] he saw himself working with God in order to eradicate the world of evil. Walton, in *The Political Philosophy of Martin Luther King, Jr.*, makes this statement about King:

Evil exists, but it is the result of man's misuse of his freedom, not the creation of God. King saw the history of man as the struggle between good and evil. Every religion recognizes that tensions in the world are caused by conflict between the forces of justice and injustice: each realizes that in the upper thrusts of goodness there is the downward pull of evil. He insisted that one of the major tenets of Christianity is the idea that in the long struggle between good and evil, good will eventually triumph. Evil is doomed by the consistent and inexorable forces of good.[30]

The church, as King explicitly understood it, was the only beacon of hope for people suffering under the crushing weight of unjust socio-economic and political policies that offered them no way of escape. undaunted by the reality of the threats to his person and the pain he certainly suffered and continued to suffer throughout his tenure as leader of the Civil Rights Movement seeking justice on behalf of the disinherited, he continued unabated in his efforts despite the harsh criticism from his detractors:

> The Christian faith makes it possible for us nobly to accept that which cannot be changed, and to meet disappointment and sorrow with an inner poise, and to absorb the most intense pain without abandoning our sense of hope.[31]

The struggle for restitution on behalf of people long denied social and economic security in their own country spearheaded his unique legacy. King's devotion to the cause and to the call could not have been made clearer than when he, in an attempt to rally a coalition of poor people in the March on Washington said,

> Those who choose to join this initial three thousand, this nonviolent army, this 'freedom church' of the poor, will work with us for three months to develop nonviolent action skills."[32]

The struggle for civil rights began centuries before Dr. King's involvement. His leadership, voice of reason and reconciliation took the struggle to successes it had never known since its inception with the arrival of Africans on the shores of America in about 1619. Early Africans soon learned the difference between slavery and freedom in America. Their struggle for liberty was and is a continuous thread of social resistance and demand by all people in America; but, especially by those then in the early stages of their presence in a land strange to them. If not for the faith, patience and courage of Dr. Martin Luther King, Jr. as a matter of humble service to God, the narrow structure of America's pre-civil rights society might still be in place today. The most dynamic push by blacks in the United States for freedom and equality came about 82 years after the emancipation Proclamation. Nearly a century was long enough for America to come to terms with its duplicity, its unmet promises, of which sweeping changes in the landmark Civil Rights legislation of 1964 and 1965, on paper, eradicated the vestiges of the shameful institution of slavery.

After these achievements, King began to fold his concerns about the Vietnam War into his Civil Rights platform. Criticisms from cynics about him addressing the war were quick and harsh. However, according to King, a protest against the war was synonymous with protests for the rights of the poor, the discriminated against, and the disenfranchised. Those conscripted to fight the war were poor boys, black and white, who had no voice in whether they should be shipped to foreign lands to engage in wars against other disenfranchised people. This stance was also a natural progression in the militancy of his preaching. As King saw it, and in fact, young black men in particular and poor white young men in general, were over represented in the army and in the jungles of Vietnam at the most active times of the war. Large numbers of disenfranchised blacks and economically deprived whites were fighting a war on the pretext of liberating a people in their nation. Those same young men—black and white—would be denied basic freedoms and liberties in their nation of America when or if they returned. On this issue, again, King had to respond to his critics. He did so from the pulpit of Ebenezer Baptist Church,

> For those who ask the question "'aren't you a civil rights leader?'"—and thereby mean to exclude me from the movement for peace—I answer by saying that I have worked too long and hard now against segregated public accommodations to end up segregating my moral concerns. Justice is indivisible.[33]

"King's appeal to Christian sensibilities allowed his words to germinate in the south, a bastion of religious conservatism and Christian belief. Here, the union of Christianity and Black protest was strong."[34] appropriately, we may again look back on the formation of Dr. King's character and how his ability to provoke soul-searching contemplation toward those who were the purveyors of a prejudiced society. As a son of the south, he could not escape what he often spoke of learning from both parents, "I think that my strong determination for justice comes from the very strong, dynamic personality of my father, and I would hope that the gentle aspect comes from a mother who is very gentle and sweet.[35] It is natural then, to conclude that with the influence of attentive, loving and engaged parents, Dr. Martin Luther King Jr.'s unwavering devotion to the betterment of humanity developed long before he became a major force for change on the world stage. It was through his personal religious experiences that he came to see the church as an incubator for nonviolent direct action in the struggle for justice and human rights. What better conduit was there than the Civil Rights Movement to combine his strength, dynamism and the gentility gained from his spiritual and family heritage—the "sweet side" of his personality.

A precious gift from God, Dr. King's voice and message to the world were vital influences in the grand sphere of change to the order of life in the United States. King's amazing ability to challenge others by his own commitment, his ability to take absolute abstractions on social justice and forge them into functional realities for everyone in the country is a stark contrast to today's narcissist leaders, who more often than not seek personal aggrandizement and material reward rather than the greater good for all. To this idea, King said, "if you are cut down in a movement that is designed to save the soul of a nation, then no other death could be more redemptive."[36] King, in writing about the civil rights activities in Birmingham in 1963, during the so called "summer of discontent", said, "With initial success, every social revolution simultaneously does two things: it attracts to itself fresh force and strength, and at the same time it crystallizes the opposition."[37] The ultimate measure of King's success was his ability to get others to buy into and garner the courage to surge ahead even when success appeared far away. Let us each remain grateful that King had a "sweet side."

CHAPTER NINE

By This Shall We Be Known: Where do we go from here?

—— ✳ ——

"If you lose hope, somehow you lose the vitality that keeps life moving, you lose that courage to be, that quality that helps you to go on in spite of all. And so today I still have a dream."[180]
Martin Luther King, Jr.

IN AN ATTEMPT TO interpret the vision, voice and message of Dr. King for the 21st century, it is important to focus on several of the issues in which he found enormously important during the later years of his life. Dr. King and the southern Christian leadership Conference (SCLC) directed their attention on three fronts or what might be called three urgent programs: "the political reformation of the south," a reconstruction of youth through meaningful training and education," and, most important, the organizing of "the poor in a crusade to reform society in order to realize economic and social justice.[181]

Most Americans, of all racial, ethnic backgrounds and cultures generally want the same thing. They want to live in a safe and secure society, free from the threat of violence and immorality, a society open to social and economic opportunities. The question most pressing of course is the realization of any of these desired programs or aims possible, with current political parties constantly bickering over political posturing, and power brokering with special interest groups? Today more than ever, this nation is starving for the calm sea of human decency and civility from its elected leaders and public servants. It is apparent that the battles of yesteryears are not so far removed. King's vision, voice and message yet rings with profound urgency within the earshot of those longing for a just and humane society. The need to train and educate young people, the political reformation that began in the south but has since help shape the political landscape of the present; and the campaign to address the economic and social justice issues, all three still have contemporary significance.

Political Protest & Mass Demonstrations

While millions of Americans annually pause to honor the memory of Dr. Martin Luther King Jr., on the national holiday named in his honor, they do so now in a post-911 world. Today, more than ever before we need to reflect on this prolific leader's life, his philosophy of nonviolent peaceful protest and his work as a prophet of peace, in a world seemingly more violent and less civil. The words of Jesus "Blessed are the peacemakers, for they will be called children of God" could not be more relevant to this 20th century prophet of peace. King's earliest work took place in the south, it later went north, throughout various cities in America. He was enveloped in the fierce violence of bombings and brutal beatings, his message of peace remained intact. "King said, I am no doctrinaire pacifist, but I have tried to embrace a realistic pacifism which finds the pacifist position as the lesser evil to the circumstances."[182] While King's words must be understood in the historical context of national and international events of his day, many Americans no doubt will reflect on Dr. King's life from the prism of Sept. 11, 2001 and the subsequent war on terrorism. It is difficult to imagine Dr. King's total response to the terrorist attacks on America; however I'm sure he, like all of us, would have been deeply distressed and appalled by such evil acts of violence. Dr. King's work in America sought to rid the world of violence and injustice, and his message of love, justice and peace still represents a symbol of what is best in our nation and our world. The patriotism that united us as a people following 9/11 gave all Americans the opportunity to experience, in some small measure, the "beloved community" ideal espoused by Dr. King.

Now, the real challenge facing our nation is, will we continue to work together for a united American democracy and civility both home and abroad, or will we maintain the disposition of the status quo of an uncivil discord? Unfortunately, hate and separatist groups are alive and well in America and throughout the globe. In America we've seen the rise of groups such as the White Christian identity Movement and the new Black Panther Movement for self-Defense, who cloak their philosophies under the banner of ethno-centric, self-determination ideology, who in truth are very divisive in purpose and nature. They hinder efforts toward national unity and are sad reminders that Dr. King's vision of a beloved community is far from being realized. Any religious or political extremist group seeking to perpetuate a doctrine of hate and discrimination is a persistent threat to American democracy and should not go unchallenged by freedom—and peace-loving people from all walks of life.

President Abraham Lincoln spoke eloquently in his famous Gettysburg address, when he said, "a new nation, conceived in liberty, and dedicated to the proposition that all men are created equal. Now we are engaged in a great civil war, testing whether that nation or any nation so conceived and so dedicated, can long endure."[183] if our nation is to move in the direction of peace, we must broaden and deepen our commitment to nonviolence, social justice and human rights. We must not be a nation that merely tolerates others who may be different; we must seek to understand others by respecting each individual's humanity under the rule of law. We must foster academic dialog. Such dialog may mean we will not always agree with the assumptions and conclusions drawn by others, but it will provide a civil environment in which to work toward more positive ends.

Dr. King ended his famous I Have A Dream speech, declaring, "...let freedom ring. And when we allow freedom to ring, when we let it ring from every village and hamlet, from every state and city, we will be able to speed up the day when all of God's children—black men and white men, Jews and Gentiles, Catholics and Protestants—will be able to join hands and to sing in the words of the old Negro spiritual, 'Free at last, free at last; thank God almighty, we are free at last.'" Of course true freedom does not come without great sacrifice. The poetic tone and substance of King's words cannot substitute for the harsh reality and difficult challenge and work needed to bring about such freedom. Again I quote President Lincoln in the Gettysburg address:

> The world will little note, nor long remember, what we say here, but it can never forget what they did here. It is for us the living, rather, to be dedicated here to the unfinished work which they who fought here have thus far so nobly advanced. It is rather for us to be here dedicated to the great task remaining before us; that from these honored dead we take increased devotion to that cause for which they gave the last full measure of devotion; that we here highly resolved that these dead shall not have died in vain, that this nation, under God, shall have a new birth of freedom; and that government of the people, for the people, shall not perish from the earth.[184]

While we must conclude that war may be viewed by many as a necessary weapon for freedom, we must seek to avoid the glorification of war. We must understand that war always comes at an immense, though often unavoidable, price. Dr. King once said, "...nobody can win a war. The choice today is no longer between violence and nonviolence. It is either nonviolence or nonexistence."

in a world of nuclear, biological and high-tech weaponry, one could argue that the reality of war makes it extremely difficult to reconcile Dr. King's vision of a beloved community. Nevertheless, like Dr. King, our hope too must rest in the teachings of Jesus Christ, who declared, "Blessed are you when others revile you and persecute you and utter all kinds of evil against you falsely on my account. Rejoice and be glad, for your reward is great in heaven, for so they persecuted the prophets who were before you." (Matt. 5:11—12 ESV)

The Constitution of the United States is the most thoroughgoing treatise on human rights in the history of modern civilization. Within it, citizens of the country are guaranteed "certain inalienable rights." among these are the right to free speech and the right of lawful assembly. In America, the Vietnam War inspired all kinds of anti-war dissent: terrorism, military desertion and collective protests, the likes of which have not been staged since, until and amid the rattled sabers of the war against Iraq, and ultimately war on terrorism. Despite the fervor of dissent against war in Iraq, it is doubtful that among the protesters any will be found who personally favored the oppressive dictatorship of Saddam Hussein and his band of henchmen. Rather, there are numerous larger issues that accompany peaceful protests, the roots of which may well be unfathomable. First, the exercise of free speech by Americans against the use of large-scale military force to depose Hussein or his corrupt dictator is a double-edged sword. On the one hand, the protests reaffirm the viability of the democratic processes in America. Protesters demand political forthrightness and most, if not all, have a visceral and passionate concern for the sanctity of human life. Yet, Americans either knowingly or unknowingly join their voices with those often here and abroad that may be distinctly violently anti-American.

Also, unfortunately, these events of lawful American assembly and free speech grant the petty dictators at the center of these peaceful yet vocal assemblies the momentary privilege of cloaking himself in the very benefits of freedom and democracy they routinely deny millions of their own countrypersons. Still further, to inadvertently coddle the enemy disavows the high value and worth of service rendered to the united states by American military personnel. Politically speaking, the right to descent has often been a controversial maneuver for political retort and engagement.

It must be noted that the right to protest by peaceful demonstrations provided King and his followers the ideal opportunity to express contempt for the unjust practice of discrimination and social segregation, as well as the immorality of the Vietnam War during the civil rights era. Today, almost every political or social action group uses similar methods to some degree or another to trumpet their cause. For example, depending on which scientific polls are believed, not all Americans or much of the rest of the world were convinced by the passions of President George Bush, secretary Powell and Prime Minister Blair for war against Iraq. Their persuasive discourses did not fully make the case that Hussein was enough of a clear and present threat to the United States and its allies to prosecute a major war against that nation. according to CNN, on Feb. 15, 2003 anti-war demonstrations were held in as many as 600 U.S. cities and 60 nations, 30 million people worldwide, including 1 million people in Britain demonstrated against the war.[185] But in that surging wave of mass human discontent, what is most at stake for America? Certainly, with or without war against Iraq, America had hundreds of thousands of lives of its military men and women at stake. Yet, under not one circumstance can the terms of democracy as provided by the Constitution of the United States for free speech and freedom of assembly be breached.

In Dan Caravale's January 31, 2003 article in The Chronicle of higher education, a statement released by the association of American universities said, "For universities to fulfill obligations to academic freedom and intellectual development, they must provide a forum in which individuals and groups can advocate their views."[186] This assertion applies equally to every American in or out of the universities. nonetheless, as Americans freely exercise their constitutional freedoms, care must be taken to balance this most delicate liberty with a healthy dose of responsibility, wisdom, forethought and an understanding of spherical consequences where America's most important military resource—the men and women in uniform—is concerned. It would go well with all Americans if those who protest chose their battles thoughtfully and carefully. Americans must take care and responsibility with protesting military action. King viewed the war in Vietnam as an unjust war. He encouraged young people to an alternative solution in opposition to fighting in that war, conscientious objection. King even praised the famous boxer Muhammad Ali's conscientious resistance to military service.[187] Ali's decision to do so cost him dearly. He was arrested and charged as a draft dodger. He was also stripped of his professional boxing rights at the peak of his career. King said "These are the times for real choices and not false ones. We are at the moment when our lives must be placed on the line if our nation is to survive its own folly. Every man of humane convictions must decide on the protest that best suits his convictions, but we all must protest."[188] On the other hand, for those who choose to serve our nation in battle, let the protest be against the policy and not against those who wear the American uniform. Richard Lischer is correct in saying, "Occasionally, politicians claim God's blessings upon selected wars, but the word "God" functions only as a cipher for the national interest. When God is mentioned at all, it is not a god we know."[189] Both policy makers and protestors must take serious the act of war, because ultimately, the consequences of war will not lie in some remote and barren war arena. The consequences will appear on American soil when men and women in uniform return home after obeying orders to perform their duties lawfully as are therein described in the Constitution of the United States of America to protect the liberties of this nation.

King elevated his thinking regarding the merits of war when he said, "War, horrible as it is, might be preferable to surrender to a totalitarian system. But I now believe that the potential destructiveness of modern weapons totally rules out the possibility of war ever again achieving a negative good."[190] King came to believed that there was always an alternative to war. The beloved community can only be realized, as Dr. King believed, when all humanity resolves "to overcome fear through faith, when humankind will overcome oppression and violence without resorting to violence and oppression." let us continue to hope, in the spirit of the Civil Rights song, "...we shall live in peace, one day."

Training and the Education of youth

In the education arena, King's vision of social reform and transformation was plainly stated in a speech he gave to the urban league in the early 60's. He said:

> We must constantly stimulate our youth to rise above the stagnant level of mediocrity and seek to achieve excellence in the various fields of endeavor. Doors are opening now that were not open in the past, and the great challenge facing minority groups is to be ready to enter these doors as they open. No great tragedy could befall us at this hour but that of allowing new opportunities to emerge without the concomitant preparedness to meet them.[191]

Today in many places the state of educational progress might well be summed up in the words of the prolific Harlem poet, Langston Hughes, "a dream deferred", or even lost, particularly in the south. The south was the very place of King's birth, the place where he invested his blood, sweat and tears. in the early 1930's, Carter G. Woodson, the renowned African American social historian wrote in his classical work, "The Mis-Education of the Negro" "if Negro [black] institutions are to be as efficient as those for the whites in the south the same high standard for the educators to direct them should be maintained."[192] There are some 106 Historically Black Colleges and Universities (HBCUs) in 24 states mostly located in the southern region of the U.S.[193] The most recent findings of the state of Historically Black Colleges and Universities (HBCUs) are disheartening. "Now only 1 in 5 black students earn bachelor's degrees from historical black schools, which have increasingly become dependent upon marginal students from poor families."[194] These words of Woodson at the beginning of the 20th century; spoken well before the pre-civil rights era of the 50's and 60's, Woodson argued that not only has the white American been educated to regard blacks as inferior, but the thinking of blacks themselves have been influenced through school and college so that they regard themselves as inferior. He said, "in this particular respect, 'Negro [black] education' is a failure, and disastrously so, because in its present predicament the race is especially in need of vision and invention to give humanity something new."[195]

Bill Maxwell, a longtime St Petersburg Times columnist, shares a similar concern today, as Woodson observed back then in the 1930's. Maxwell revealed in a series of three newspaper articles, the disappointing reality of education in many of the Historically Black Colleges and Universities; located mostly in the south. As a professionally trained journalist and product of Historically Black College educational system, Maxwell wanted to give back by mentoring and nurturing young people in a similar way, in which he was mentored and nurtured. In the fall of 2005, he left the St. Petersburg Times, and spent two years teaching journalism on the campus of Stillman College in Tuscaloosa, Alabama. Stillman, founded in 1876, is one of many HBCUs, and established to train and educate the black population in the south. The enrollment of this small rural college is approximately 1,000 students. Maxwell chronicled his experience. In his first article appropriately titled: "I had a Dream" he details his feelings at the end of a semester of teaching:

> Each time, I would leave the English class exhausted, angry and sad. I would go home on many evenings during my first month wanting to cry, and things didn't get much better as the year progressed. I had come to Stillman on the mission of my life: I wanted to be of use, to help "uplift the race" as my professors had taught me. But as my first school year ended in the spring, instead of feeling useful and as if I were helping to uplift the race, I was feeling helpless and irrelevant.[196]

As Maxwell chronicles his experiences as a teacher who wanted to make a positive difference in the lives of students at this historical Black College, ultimately he became discouraged to the point of giving up and returning to his prior profession as a journalist for the Times. He writes, "By the end of the spring; I knew that I could not remain at Stillman another year. I had a few good students, but a few were not enough. One morning as I dressed for work, I accepted the reality that too much of my time was being wasted on students who did not care."[197]

While Maxwell's experience on Stillman's campus only represents one perspective, unfortunately the statistics reveal the achievement levels of many historical Black Colleges and universities is much too low. In fact, the 6-year graduation rate at Stillman is 29 percent. The 6 year graduation rate at the University of Alabama is 63 percent. The 6 year graduation rate at FAMU is 33 percent, and the 6 year graduation rate Florida State is at 66 percent.[198] Certainly, Dr. King's vision for high educational standards demanded a tremendous amount of personal responsibility from students and teachers. He said, "We must make it clear to our young people that this is an age in which they will be forced to compete with people of all races and nationalities. We cannot aim merely to be good [black] teachers, good black doctors, or good black skilled laborers. We must set out to do a good job irrespective of race."[199] in Maxwell's second article titled: A Dream Lay Dying, he wrote "My colleagues and I were witnessing the result of low admission standards. Were we expecting too much of young people who scored poorly on the SAT, who were rarely challenged to excel in high school, who were not motivated to take advantage of opportunities to learn, who could not imagine where a sound education could take them?"[200]

Just as Carter G. Woodson had revealed some hard and disappointing truths of his day, so did Maxwell, who's critique of the academic standards at Stillman is most telling, he said, "For many, the rappers Bow Wow and 50 Cent were at least as important to black achievement as the late Ralph Bunche, the first black to win a Nobel Peace Prize, and Zora Neale Hurston, the great novelist.[201] In spite of the fact that Maxwell left Stillman out of sheer frustration he says "I cannot turn my back on these schools. I cannot forget what they did for me many years ago, and I cannot forget the handful of dedicated students at Stillman who were determined to succeed even in the face of the school's considerable shortcomings.[202] It must not be overlooked that the Reverend Dr. Martin Luther King, Jr., is the product of a Historically Black College, Morehouse College in Atlanta, Georgia. Bill Maxwell is careful to point out that "the top-tier [HBCUs], these schools will continue to attract good students and remain vibrant, financially viable institutions. Among those familiar names are Spellman College and Morehouse College in Atlanta and Howard University in Washington, D.C., each a member of the so-called "Black Ivy League.""[203] By the time Maxwell completed his series of articles his conclusion was clear that much remains be done if King's dream is to fully be realized in the education arena.

Today, the failing of American education is not limited to Historical Black Colleges and Universities or to only minority students. Current stats reveal that the high school dropout rate is at an all-time high. "Today's report confirms that our nation faces a dropout crisis. When 25 percent of our students—and almost 40 percent of our black and Hispanic students—fail to graduate high school on time, we know that too many of our schools are failing to offer their students a world-class education."[204] Fewer students are leaving school prepared to contribute to the betterment of society. In a speech entitled, "Facing the Challenge of a new age," given December 1956, at the First Annual Institute on Non-Violence and Social Change in Montgomery, Alabama, King said,

> "We must set out to do a good job, irrespective of race, and do it so well that nobody can do it better whatever your life's work is, do it well. Even if it does not fall in the category of one of the so-called big professions, do it well. As one college president said, "a man should do his job so well that the living, the dead, and the unborn could do it no better." If it falls your lot to be a street sweeper, sweep streets like

Michelangelo painted pictures, like Shakespeare wrote poetry, like Beethoven composed music; sweep streets so well that all the host of heaven and earth will have to pause and say, "Here lived a great street sweeper, who swept his job well."[205]

The Poor Peoples Campaign

As the shifting tumultuous ocean tide, the billowing currents of King's swift broad new program emphasis burst forth. In addressing the SCLC staff, a year prior to his death King said, "We must formulate a program, and we must fashion new tactics which do not count on government good will, but instead serve to compel unwilling authorities to yield to the mandates of justice."[206] There were noteworthy accomplishments and legislative achievements during the Civil Rights Movement of the 60's such as passage of the Civil Rights Act of 1964 that banned discrimination based on "race, color, religion, or national origin" in employment practices and public accommodations. In fact, President Johnson declared, "the 1964 Civil Rights act as further fulfillment of the ideals of the Declaration of independence, which 'a small band of valiant men' had signed 188 years earlier.[207] Also the Voting Rights act of 1965 restored and protected voting rights. "Enforcement of the 1965 Voting Rights act too brought swift initial results. Within two years, several hundred thousand black citizens had been added to the voter rolls in six southern states.[208] and finally the Fair Housing Act of 1968 that banned discrimination in the sale or rental of housing passed after King's assassination but was something he'd fought hard for during his lifetime.[209] even with the legislative successes, King was determined to address the systematic issues of economic injustice. according to King, "among the goals must be guaranteed annual income and the elimination of slums.[210] King's last Sunday morning sermon: Remaining awake Through a Great Revolution provides a clear window into his thoughts on poverty, where in dramatic oratorical fashion he paints the picture using the story of the rich man Dives and the poor man Lazarus as found in Luke's gospel. King said "this is America's opportunity to help bridge the gulf between the haves and the have-nots. The question is whether America will do it."[211] There is nothing new about poverty. What is new is that we now have the techniques and the resources to get rid of poverty. The real question is whether we have the will.[212] Both the Hebrew and Christian scripture remind us of the ever present reality of poverty. He who oppresses the poor to increase his wealth and he who gives gifts to the rich—both come to poverty (Prov. 22:16). The LORD sends poverty and wealth; he humbles and he exalts (I Sam. 2:7). For you know the grace of our lord Jesus Christ, that though he was rich, yet for your sakes he became poor, so that you through his poverty might become rich (2 Cor. 8:9). I know your afflictions and your poverty—yet you are rich! I know the slander of those who say they are Jews and are not, but are a synagogue of Satan (Rev. 2:9).

Howard Thurman in his classic work, *Jesus and the Disinherited*, suggest "The economic predicament with which [Jesus] was identified in birth placed him initially with the great mass of [people] on earth. The masses of the people are poor.[213] as Ruby K. Payne points out in her work *A Framework for Understanding Poverty*, "poverty occurs in all races and in all countries."[214] While King was well aware of the effects of poverty on blacks as the result of discrimination, he was also aware that being poor, transcended race. King said, "in the treatment of poverty nationally, one fact stands out: there are twice as many white poor as [black] poor in the United States. Therefore I will not dwell on the experiences of poverty that derived from racial discrimination, but will discuss the poverty that affects white and [black] alike.[215] Current data suggest, "While the number of Caucasian children in poverty is the largest group, the percentage of children in poverty in most minority groups is higher.[216] The implication being that even the soul redeemer of humanity understood and identified with the plight of the poor. Payne emphasizes the point that poverty must be understood in context beyond the financial resources. She suggests, "The ability to leave poverty is more dependent upon other resources than it is upon financial resources."[217] her list includes the following: emotional, mental, spiritual, physical, support systems, and relationship/role model resources all play a significant role in helping one rise above poverty.[218] The reality is poverty is tremendous burden which adversely impacts millions of lives daily. The fact that the "united states' child poverty rate is substantially higher—often two or three times higher—than that of most other major Western industrialized nations" is room to be concerned.[219]

According to Center for American Progress 2007 Task Force on Poverty "Thirty-seven million Americans live below the official poverty line. Millions more struggle each month to pay for basic necessities, or run out of savings when they lose their jobs or face health emergencies.[220] At the beginning of the 21st century, King's program on poverty and commitment to economic justice could not be more relevant. In 2009, "employers shed 539,000 jobs in April, and while this is down from the past few months, it remains the ninth-largest one month fall in employment since the end of World War II. The economy has shed 5.7 million jobs since the recession began in December 2007…"[221]

In 2007 the Center for American Progress proposed a strategy to cut poverty in half over the next 10 years. The strategy consisted of the following four guiding principles:

1. Promote Decent Work. People should work and work should pay enough to ensure that workers and their families can avoid poverty, meet basic needs, and save for the future.

2. Provide opportunity for all. Children should grow in conditions that maximize their opportunities for success; adults should have opportunities throughout their lives to connect to work, get more education, live in a good neighborhood, and move up in the workforce.

3. Ensure economic security. Americans should not fall into poverty when they cannot work or work is unavailable, unstable, or pays so little that they cannot make ends meet.

4. Help people Build Wealth. all Americans should have the opportunity to build assets that allow them to weather periods of flux and volatility, and to have the resources that may be essential to advancement and upward mobility.[222]

The Taskforce on Poverty provided a very bold and broad strategy which does get at the root of many King's concerns. King said the assistant director of the office of economic opportunity, Hyman Bookbinder, in December 1966 said, "That the long-range costs of adequate implementing programs to fight poverty, ignorance and slums will reach one trillion dollars. He was not awed or dismayed by this prospect but instead pointed out that the growth of the gross national product during the same period makes this expenditure comfortably possible."[223] according to the 2007 Taskforce on Poverty, "The combined cost of our principle recommendations is in the range of $90 billion a year—a significant cost but one that could be readily funded through a fairer tax system. An additional $90 billion in annual spending would represent about 0.8 percent of the nation's gross domestic product."[224] according to Taskforce on Poverty the urban institutes, which modeled implementation of one set of the recommendations, estimates that four of the steps would reduce poverty by 26 percent, bringing us halfway toward the 10 year goal to cut poverty in half? The following is a list of recommendations and finding of the Taskforce on Poverty:

We recommend 12 key steps to cut poverty in half:

1. Raise and index the minimum wage to half the average hourly wage. At $5.15, the federal minimum wage is at its lowest level in real terms since 1956. The federal minimum wage was once 50 percent of the average wage but is now 30 percent of that wage. Congress should restore the minimum wage to 50 percent of the average wage, about $8.40 an hour in 2006. Doing so would help nearly 5 million poor workers and nearly 10 million other low-income workers.

2. Expand the earned income Tax Credit and Child Tax
    Credit. As an earnings supplement for low-income working
    families, the EITC raises incomes and helps families build
    assets. The Child Tax Credit provides a tax credit of up
    to $1,000 per child, but provides no help to the poorest
    families. We recommend tripling the EITC for childless
    workers and expanding help to larger working families. We
    recommend making the Child Tax Credit available to all
    low—and moderate-income families. Doing so would move
    as many as 5 million people out of poverty.

3. Promote unionization by enacting the employee Free Choice
    act. The employee Free Choice act would require employers
    to recognize a union after a majority of workers signs cards
    authorizing union representation and establish stronger
    penalties for violation of employee rights. The increased
    union representation made possible by the act would lead to
    better jobs and less poverty for American workers.

4. Guarantee child care assistance to low-income families and
    promote early education for all. We propose that the federal
    and state governments guarantee child care help to families
    with incomes below about $40,000 a year, with expanded
    tax help to higher-earning families. At the same time,
    states should be encouraged to improve the quality of early
    education and broaden access for all children. Our child
    care expansion would raise employment among low-income
    parents and help nearly 3 million parents and children
    escape poverty.

5. Create 2 million new "opportunity" housing vouchers, and
    promote equitable development in and around central
    cities. Nearly 8 million Americans live in neighborhoods of
    concentrated poverty where at least 40 percent of residents
    are poor. Our nation should seek to end concentrated
    poverty and economic segregation, and promote regional
    equity and inner-city revitalization. We propose that over

the next 10 years the federal government fund 2 million new "opportunity vouchers" designed to help people live in opportunity-rich areas. Any new affordable housing should be in communities with employment opportunities and high-quality public services, or in gentrifying communities. These housing policies should be part of a broader effort to pursue equitable development strategies in regional and local planning efforts, including efforts to improve schools, create affordable housing, assure physical security, and enhance neighborhood amenities.

6. Connect disadvantaged and disconnected youth with school and work. About 1.7 million poor youth ages 16 to 24 were out of school and out of work in 2005. We recommend that the federal government restore youth opportunity Grants to help the most disadvantaged communities and expand funding for effective and promising youth programs—with the goal of reaching 600,000 poor disadvantaged youth through these efforts. We propose a new upward Pathway program to offer low-income youth opportunities to participate in service and training in fields that are in high-demand and provide needed public services.

7. Simplify and expand Pell Grants and make higher education accessible to residents of each state. Low-income youth are much less likely to attend college than their higher income peers, even among those of comparable abilities. Pell Grants play a crucial role for lower-income students. We propose to simplify the Pell grant application process, gradually raise Pell Grants to reach 70 percent of the average costs of attending a four-year public institution, and encourage institutions to do more to raise student completion rates. As the federal government does its part, states should develop strategies to make postsecondary education affordable for all residents, following promising models already underway in a number of states.

8. Help former prisoners find stable employment and reintegrate into their communities. The United States has the highest incarceration rate in the world. We urge all states to develop comprehensive reentry services aimed at reintegrating former prisoners into their communities with full-time, consistent employment.

9. Ensure equity for low-wage workers in the Unemployment Insurance system. Only about 35 percent of the unemployed, and a smaller share of unemployed low-wage workers, receive unemployment insurance benefits. We recommend that states (with federal help) reform "monetary eligibility" rules that screen out low-wage workers, broaden eligibility for part-time workers and workers who have lost employment as a result of compelling family circumstances, and allow unemployed workers to use periods of unemployment as a time to upgrade their skills and qualifications.

10. Modernize means-tested benefits programs to develop a coordinated system that helps workers and families. A well-functioning safety net should help people get into or return to work and ensure a decent level of living for those who cannot work or are temporarily between jobs. Our current system fails to do so. We recommend that governments at all levels simplify and improve benefits access for working families and improve services to individuals with disabilities. The Food stamp Program should be strengthened to improve benefits, eligibility, and access. And the Temporary Assistance for Needy Families Program should be reformed to shift its focus from cutting caseloads to helping needy families find sustainable employment.

11. Reduce the high costs of being poor and increase access to financial services. Despite having less income, lower-income families often pay more than middle and high-income families for the same consumer products. We recommend that the federal and state governments should

address the foreclosure crisis through expanded mortgage assistance programs and by new federal legislation to curb unscrupulous practices. And we propose that the federal government establish a $50 million Financial Fairness innovation Fund to support state efforts to broaden access to mainstream goods and financial services in predominantly low-income communities.

12. Expand Saver's Credit and simplify opportunities that encourage saving for education, homeownership, and retirement. For many families, saving for purposes such as education, a home, or a small business is key to making economic progress. We propose that the federal "Saver's Credit" be reformed to make it fully refundable. This Credit should also be broadened to apply to other appropriate savings vehicles intended to foster asset accumulation, with consideration given to including individual development accounts, children's saving accounts, and college savings plans.

Our recommendations would cut poverty in half. The urban institute, which modeled the implementation of one set of our recommendations, estimates that four of our steps would reduce poverty by 26 percent, bringing us more than halfway toward our goal. Among their findings:

- Taken together, our minimum wage, EITC, child credit, and child care recommendations would reduce poverty by 26 percent. This would mean 9.4 million fewer people in poverty and a national poverty rate of 9.1 percent—the lowest in recorded U.S. history.

- The racial poverty gap would be narrowed: White poverty would fall from 8.7 percent to 7 percent. Poverty among African Americans would fall from 21.4 percent to 15.6 percent. Hispanic poverty would fall from 21.4 percent to 12.9 percent and poverty for all others would fall from 12.7 percent to 10.3 percent.

- Child poverty and extreme poverty would both fall: Child poverty would drop by 41 percent. The number of people in extreme poverty would fall by 2.4 million.

- Millions of low—and moderate-income families would benefit. Almost half of the benefits of our proposal would help low—and moderate-income families.

- That these recommendations would reduce poverty by more than one quarter is powerful evidence that a 50 percent reduction can be reached within a decade.[225]

It is noteworthy to now reflect back on the plans of Martin Luther King, Jr. and the southern Christian leaderships to address the issue of poverty. King and his comrades decided to organize a Poor People Campaign with a march on Washington much different from the august 1963 march. "This time the purpose would not be 'to have a beautiful day,' King said, but literally to occupy the city until the Johnson administration altered both its domestic and foreign policy.[226] It was obvious that King believed that the first March on Washington did not achieve its ultimate aims or at least the momentum had been lost, due primarily to the shift of political focus to the War in Vietnam. "Two days after the retreat, King held a press conference to announce SCLC's plans. 'Waves of the nation's poor and disinherited' would descend upon Washington around April 1, and 'will stay until America responds' with 'specific reforms,…until some definite and positive actions is taken to provide jobs and income for the poor.",[227] The real battle today should be making sure the doors remain open so that others of any ethnic or racial group will have access to the opportunities made possible by a free market society. The legacy of the Civil Rights Movement is to ensure equal opportunity and equal access to the American dream.

Pictured on left, Dr. Terriel Byrd with Reverend Fred
Shuttlesworth in the pulpit of the Greater New Light
Baptist Church, Cincinnati, Ohio

Dr. Byrd and Reverend Shuttlesworth standing in church
foyer

Street sign in Cincinnati honoring the legendary Civil
Rights leader, Fred Shuttlesworth
Well done good and faith servant!
In memory March 8, 1922—October 5, 2011

CHAPTER TEN

Closing Reflections: Martin Luther King Jr.'s Vision, Voice and Message Live On!

✳

"Then the pilgrims got up and walked to and fro; but how were their ears now filled with heavenly noises, and their eyes delighted with celestial visions!"[228] *John Bunyan*

IT IS DIFFICULTY TO fully comprehend the Civil Rights Movement of the 1950's and 60's without taking into account the tremendous role the black church played in shaping the course in which its leaders took. The movement was identified by a creative and cohesive spirit of solidarity. The black church chose Martin Luther King as its primary leader and stood with him and his staff through the darkest and most difficult hours of the challenge presented to them by the struggles and demands for civil and social justice in America.

This work observed that role and the influence of the church and Martin Luther King, Jr. from the vantage of this spiritual environment. It examined how King and the Church placed themselves in a position of dependence on God's Grace to achieve what then seemed like unattainable goals. The core inspiration for this book came from the overlooked aspects of ecclesial and scholarly investigations into the spiritual ethos and faith commitments that were central elements, and the motivation of Dr. King and other pioneers of the Civil Rights Movement. To them, the evils of racism, segregation and disenfranchisement of half the nation emanated from the malevolent hearts of men. After all, it was Christ who said that it is not what goes into a man that makes him unclean, but what comes from his heart and through his mouth that makes him unclean. Dr. King's determination of a spiritual trajectory and discourse on the problems of race encompassed a strong spiritual focus. For this aspect of his philosophy to remain overlooked would continue as an amazing lapse of accuracy in the historical record, in as much as American Christianity including that brand of faith which is practiced by the black church had a specific influence on the Civil Rights movement.

I was only twelve years of age at the time of Dr. King's tragic death; however, in the mid-eighties while serving as a campus minister at Miami University in Ohio, I was privileged to be introduced to one of Dr. King's closest Civil Rights comrades, Reverend Fred Shuttlesworth. This one time meeting ultimately developed into a lasting friendship that has lasted until now.

In the late eighties I was elected to serve as senior pastor of Inspirational Baptist Church in Cincinnati Ohio, in the same city where after death threats to his life, Reverend Shuttlesworth relocated after leaving Birmingham, Alabama. Occasionally, we came in contact through the Ministerial alliance association of which we were both members. I admired the worked he continued to do in the area of civil and human rights, specifically the Grant assistance the Shuttlesworth Foundation gave to low income families and first time home buyers.[229]

I always looked forward to Reverend Shuttlesworth's standing invitation to me to preach during his church's anniversary celebration. In my conversations with Reverend Shuttlesworth regarding his time spent with Dr. King, he'd always return to a common assessment of the Civil Rights leader: Dr. King had a new and different voice, unlike that of any past civil rights leaders. Frankly, I felt extremely honored to be invited by such a noted Civil Rights leader and King associate. After all, it was Fred Shuttlesworth who urged Dr. King and the Southern Christian Leadership Conference to join him and his Alabama Christian Movement for human Rights (ACMHR) organization, to come to Birmingham and challenge the notorious police Commissioner Eugene "Bull" Conner.[230] Of course, the outcome of his sojourn into Birmingham is now history! King's famous *Letter from the Birmingham Jail* and the Birmingham protest of civil disobedience helped launch the movement to greater national prominence. In fact, the media coverage around the world showed the brutality of police using fire hoses and police dogs to attack innocent nonviolent protestors, informing a naïve nation of the far-reaching problem of race in America.[231] Fred Shuttlesworth who endured beatings, home and church bombings in Birmingham, Alabama, is now honored in the same city with a Civil Rights museum and a statue of Shuttlesworth that stands as a monument and a beacon that recounts his tireless work along with Dr. King and so many others who contributed to the Civil Rights Movement of the 50's and 60's in Birmingham, Alabama and throughout the south.

It was through my friendship with Reverend Fred Shuttlesworth which provided me a first hand and personal glimpse into the world of this historical movement. Reverend Shuttlesworth shared the core values that were embodied in the movement as well as the passion and the spiritual energy that Martin Luther King and others possessed. This passion and spiritual energy was acquired from nurture through worship and fellowship, the social and spiritual commitment to the church, the place which gave sustenance to the Civil Rights Movement.

By This Shall You Be Known has sought to bring to light the multi-layered aspects of Martin Luther King, Jr.'s life and thought, and how his public life derived primarily from the simplicity of his Christian faith, yet it fortified the depth of his preaching and his vision for humanity. His voice, vision and message permeated the twentieth century and none has been stronger and more influential in shaping the world's contemporary understanding of the potential role of the church and how persons of faith can and must play a role in the struggle for social justice and human rights. The essence of King's monumental success, is that without the Black Church there likely would not have been such a significant more powerful coalition of the Civil Rights Movement; conversely, without Martin Luther King's powerful, passionate preaching there might not have been such a significant and focused twentieth century political movement for social justice which originated within the Black Christian Church, and was supportive of this monumental and lasting change. So, explorations of the relationship between King's vision, voice and message are essential to understanding the great social changes that have shaped, and will continue to shape the post postmodern world well into the 21st century and beyond. King's vision for social equality, his voice and message of justice, and dignity give the fullest expression to the challenges now facing contemporary society in America and the world at large. The church mustn't stand idly by in the midst of social challenges. In the words of T. S. Elliot "Whether people say that the Church ought to interfere, or whether they say it ought to mind its own business, depends mostly on whether they agree with its attitude upon the issue of the moment."[232]

The Civil Rights Movement of the twentieth century represented the issue of the moment, a world changing phenomenon unlike any before it on the stage of the human struggle for equality. It was that final push in a long line of movements for racial parity that yielded the open society long sought after for all people in America. The enormity of this single accomplishment, though it had world-wide impact, however, should not overshadow the simple truths and practical wisdom that may still be gleaned from the sermons, speeches and writings of Dr. Martin Luther King, Jr. Without question, his message is still relevant today as the world traverses the bridge of the twenty first century and encounters more difficult continental and intercontinental human relations. As a result, the wisdom and passion couched in King's preaching are often sought out and repeated. His words are among the most widely quoted and reflected upon by scholars, activists and social thinkers from around the globe as the quest for peace and social freedom continues.

Martin Luther Kings' vision still provides a glimpse into a future where the church can function as an effective agent of positive change that is able also to keep the church in a state of dynamic transformation, vibrancy of worship, wholeness, social and spiritual importance.

The church remains the primary source of power and the vehicle through which the larger community's social aspirations are guided. While the black church has always been the base of political, economic and cultural activities in African American's quest for liberation, the world can now see practically how this vibrant organism can foster social justice and peace throughout the world. As Lewis Baldwin eloquently states concerning King, "he drank from the wellsprings of that curious mixture of African and European spirituality concocted in the Southern Black Baptist Church, and that institution became an important part of his religious self-understanding."[233] and as Richard Lischer notes, "in the ordered environment of the African Baptist Church King discovered his vocation and the strength to carry it out."[234]

Many have written about Kings phenomenal preaching/ speaking ability, his moral and political philosophy, his synthesis of intellectual and theological thought, but few have fully, systematically examined King's inseparable and uniquely visible relationship to the black church. Hopefully this work has ushered in this new refreshing conversation. Michael Eric Dyson in his work, *I May Not Get There With You*, provides one of the most succinct statements regarding the ecclesiology of King when he states, "If we are to understand the moral thrust behind King's ideological evolution, we have to understand the complex components of his identity. And nothing was more important in shaping his identity than the radical remnant of the black church."[235] King's life & thought must be understood with the recognition that he was a product of the church and was informed by the churches rituals and traditions. Dr. King recognized religion as a personal thing, something to be experienced and lived out. The church was vital and important, the center of spiritual activity and involvement. King's theology was one of practice. His theology was unique mixture of evangelical liberalism and social justice. He saw himself working with God in order to eradicate evil in the world.

King's redemptive prophetic radicalism embraced the biblical definition of reconciliation within the context of the black struggle for liberation. He believed that it was possible for all people to live together, to work together and be together in society. He was committed to working at achieving this togetherness. Garrow writes:

> But if one takes seriously King's ideal of Christian brotherhood and his vision of the beloved community beyond racism, oppression and injustice, then it seems to me that reconciliation between blacks and whites is a logical correlation of genuine liberation.[236]

King's concept of love represented the true source of liberation. If true liberation was to be realized it would mean the liberation of both the oppressed and the oppressor. King's vision of the beloved community ultimately meant the restoring of broken relationships within the context of the human community. Racism, discrimination and hate are the divisive weapons used to split and divide community. King called for worldwide fellowship based upon the concept of love. King put it this way:

> This call for a world-wide fellowship that lifts neighborly concerns beyond ones tribe, race, class and nation is in reality a call for an all-embracing and unconditional love for all men. This often misunderstood and misinterpreted concept has now become absolute necessity for the survival of man.[237]

King's concept of community was very much related to his biblical understanding of how God would build this "community." He saw the struggles of African Americans as part of a greater plan, that God was working throughout history in order to fulfill his divine plan. His greatest resource was always his undying faith nurtured in the spiritual rituals and traditions of the African American Church, Christ message of love and forgiveness and God's call to ministry upon his life—a ministry that began in the Church. May each of us seek such a worthy call. By this we also shall be known!

NOTES

---- ❋ ----

Prologue:
  The desclining role of the modern Civil Rights Movement:
    21st Century Challenge

1   Saint Augustine, R.P.H. Green, ed. *On Christian Teaching* (New York, Oxford University Press, 1997), 27.

Chapter one:
  King's Vision, Voice and Message of the 21st Century

2   Martin Luther King Jr., ed. by James M. Washington, *The Essential Writings and Speeches of Martin Luther King, Jr.* (New York, NY: HarperSanFrancisco, 1991), 268—69.

3   Ibid., 513.

4   Ibid., 276.

5   Amanda Logan, Tim Westrich, *"How Are Minorities Faring in the Economy?"* Center for American Progress, http://www. americanprogress. org/issues/2008/04/minorities_economy. html (14 July 2010).

Chapter Two:
Sunday Morning: Thy Kingdom Come, Thy Will Be Done

[6] Martin Luther King, Jr. Clayborne Carson, ed., *The Papers of Martin Luther King, Jr.: Vo. 1 Called to Serve January 1929—June 1951* (Berkeley & Los Angeles, California, University of California Press, 1992), 361.

[7] Lewis, Baldwin V. *There is a Balm in Gilead: the Cultural Roots of Martin Luther King, Jr.* (Minneapolis, MN: Fortress Press, 1991), 171.

[8] David L. Lewis, *King A Biography* (Chicago, University of Illinois Press, 1978), 6.

[9] Ibid., 7.

[10] Lewis, Baldwin V. *There is a Balm in Gilead*, 17.

[11] Martin Luther King, Jr. Clayborne Carson, ed., *The Autobiography of Martin Luther King, Jr.*,

[12] Martin Luther King, Jr., James Washington ed., *A Testament of Hope*, 419.

[13] Martin Luther King, Jr., *The Measure of a Man* (Minneapolis, Fortress Press, 2001), 15.

[14] Ibid., 419.

[15] Ibid., 418—19.

[16] Martin Luther King, Jr., James Washington ed., *A Testament of Hope*, 423.

[17] Taylor Branch, *Parting the Waters: America in the King Years 1954—63* (New York, Touchstone, Simon & Schuster, 1988), 25.

[18] Martin Luther King, Jr. Clayborne Carson, ed., *Autobiography of Martin Luther King, Jr.*, 56.

[19] Ibid., 60.

[20] Taylor Branch. *Parting the Waters* (New York, Simon & Schuster, 1988), 140

21 Ibid., 61.

22 Coretta Scott King, ed. Martin Luther King, Jr. *Companion: Quotations from the Speeches—Essays and Books of Martin Luther King, Jr.* (New York: St. Martins Press, 1993), 98.

23 Michael Moncur, "Quotation#24968 from Classic Quotes" 1994—2007 QuotationsPage.com, <http://www.quotationspage.com/quote/24968. Html> (7 May 2007). Martin Luther King Jr., speech in Detroit, June 23, 1963, us black civil rights leader & clergyman (1929—1968).

24 24 William Barclay, *Daily Bible Series: The Gospel of Mark, revised edition*, (Philadelphia, Westminster Press, 1975), 82.

25 NN.T. Wright, *Simply Christian* (New York, NY: Harper Collins, 2006), 56.

26 (John R. Tyson 1999), 392.

Chapter Three:
Stand up for Justice: Moral Consciousness for the 21st Century

27 Coretta Scott King, ed., *The Martin Luther King, Jr., Companion: Quotations from the Speeches, Essays, and Books of Martin Luther King, Jr.* (New York, St. Martin Press, 1993), 53.

28 Martin Luther King, Jr. *A Testament of Hope* (HarperCollins, New York, 1986), 345.

29 Cleophus J. LaRue, ed. *Power in the Pulpit: How America's Most Effective Black Preachers Prepare Their Sermons* (Louisville, Kentucky, Westminster John Knox Press, 2002), 21.

30 Hanes Walton. *The Political Philosophy of Dr. Martin Luther King, Jr.* (Greenwood Publications, West Port, Conn. 1971), 52.

31 Coretta Scott King, ed., *The Martin Luther King, Jr., Companion.* (New York, St. Martin Press, 1993), 53.

32 Martin Luther King, Jr. *The Trumpet of Conscience* (harper & Row, Publishers: New York, 1967), 60.

33 *The Trumpet of Conscience,* 24.

34 Christopher B. Strain. *Pure Fire: Self-Defense as Activism in the Civil Rights Era* (Athens, Georgia, The university of Georgia Press, 2005), 43.

35 Martin Luther King Jr., Clayborne Carson ed., *The Autobiography of Martin Luther King, Jr.* (New York, NY: Warner Books, 1998), 3.

36 Martin Luther King, Jr., Coretta Scott King, ed. *The Words of Martin Luther King, Jr.* (New York, Newmarket Press, 1987), 52.

37 Martin Luther King, Jr., *Why We Can't Wait* (New York, New York, Penguin Books, 1963), 118.

Chapter Four:
  Evangelical liberalism: Justice a social enterprise

38 Howard Thurman. *Jesus and the Disinherited* (Boston, Beacon Press, 1976), 97.

39 Martin Luther King, Jr., *Why We Can't Wait* (New York, NY: signet Books, 1964), 77.

40 Martin Luther King, Jr. *The Measure of a Man* (Minneapolis, Fortress Press, 1988), 19—21.

41 Taylor Branch, *Parting the Water: America in the King Years 1954—63* (New York: Simon & Schuster, 1988), 166.

42 Richard Lischer, *The Preacher King* (New York, NY: Oxford University Press, 1995), 12.

43 William Philpot, ed., *Best Black Sermons* (Valley Forge, Pa. Judson Press, 1972), 37.

44 Taylor Branch, *Parting the Water: America in the King Years 1954—63* (New York: Simon & Schuster, 1988), 227.

45 Lewis A. Drumond. *The Evangelist: The Worldwide Impact of Billy Graham* (Nashville, TN: Word Publishing, 2001), 188.

46   Taylor Branch. *Parting the Waters*, 227.

47   Ibid., 447.

48   Richard Lischer, *The Preacher King* (New York, NY: Oxford University Press, 1995), 7.

49   Martin Luther King, Jr. James M. Washington, ed., *A Testament of Hope* (New York, NY: HarperSanFrancisco, 1986), 448.

50   Ibid., 448.

51   Reverend Dr. Jess Moody interview, West Palm Beach, Florida. 18 April 2009. [Moody is the founding president of Palm Beach Atlantic university and former pastor of First Baptist Church West Palm Beach Florida]

52   Moody interview, 18 April, 2009.

53   Fulop and Raboteau, ed. *African-American Religion* (New York, Routledge), 358.

54   Lischer, *The Preacher King* (New York, Oxford University Press), 12.

55   David J. Garrow. *Bearing the Cross: Martin Luther King, Jr., and the Southern Christian Leadership Conference* (New York, HarperCollins, 1986), 97.

56   Richard Lischer, *The Preacher King: Martin Luther King, Jr. and The Word That Moved America* (New York, Oxford University Press, 1995), 253.

57   Martin Luther King, Jr., *The Measure of a Man* (Minneapolis, Fortress Press, 2001), 12.

58   Martin Luther King, Jr. Coretta Scott King, ed. *The Martin Luther King Companion: Quotations from the speeches, Essays and Books of Martin Luther King, Jr.* (New York, NY: St/ Martin's Press, 1993), 25.

59   Martin Luther King, Jr., *The Measure of a Man* (Minneapolis, MN: 1988), 45—46.

Chapter Five:
Redemptive Suffering: Suffering Don't Last Always!

[60] Howard Thurman. *Jesus and the Disinherited* (Boston, Ma, Beacon Press, 1976), 51.

[61] Martin Luther King, Jr., *Strength to Love* (Philadelphia, Fortress Press, 1963), 48.

[62] David J. Garrow, *Bearing the Cross: Martin Luther King, Jr. and the Southern Christian Leadership Conference* (New York, William Morrow Company, 1986), 87.

[63] Michel D. Googan, ed., *The New Oxford Annotated Bible, Third Edition* (New York, Oxford University Press, 2001), 174 [new Testament].

[64] Peter J. Ling. *Martin Luther King, Jr.* (New York, Routledge, 2002), 57.

[65] Richard Lischer. *The Preacher King* (New York, Oxford University Press, 1995), 187.

[66] Merrill Unger. *Unger's Bible Dictionary* (Chicago, IL, Moody Press, 1966), 890.

[67] *Testament of Hope,* 300.

[68] *The Preacher King,* 174.

[69] Martha J. Simmons, ed., *Preaching On the Brink* (Nashville, Abingdon Press, 1996), 156.

[70] Walter Brueggeman, The non-negotiable Price of sanity, Journal for Preachers, advent 2004.

[71] Partial transcript of comments from the September 13, 2001 telecast of the 700 Club. http://www.actupny.org/yell/falwell.html 04/13/09.

[72] Gustave Niebuhr, U.S. 'secular' groups set Tone for Terror attacks, Falwell says. New York Times, September 14, 2001, http://www. nytimes.com 04/13/2009.

73   Carson Clayborne, ed. *The Autobiography of Martin Luther King, Jr.* (New York, Time Warner Books, 1998), 338.

74   Martin Luther King, Jr. *Strength to Love* (Philadelphia, Fortress Press, 1963), 132.

75   Michael Eric Dyson. *April 4, 1968: Martin Luther King, Jr.'s Death and How it Changed America* (New York, Basic Civitas Books, 2008), 34.

76   PBs, Bill Moyer, "now with Bill Moyer society and Community: Faith in America" http://www.pbs.org/now/society/religionstats.html (9 March, 2009).

77   *Testament of Hope*, 219.

78   *Testament of Hope*, 286.

79   *The Autobiography of Martin Luther King, Jr.* (New York, Time Warner Books, 1998), 77—78.

80   Lewis Baldwin, *There is a Balm in Gilead* (Minneapolis, Fortress Press; 1991), 240.

81   Martin Luther King, Jr. *Strength to Love* (Philadelphia, Fortress Press, 1963), 48.

82   Stanley Hauerwas. *The Peaceable Kingdom* (Notre Dame Indiana, University of Notre Dame Press, 1983), 87.

83   *The Preacher King*, 174.

84   Lewis V. Baldwin. *There is a Balm in Gilead: The Cultural Roots of Martin Luther King, Jr.* (Minneapolis, Fortress Press, 1991), 77.

85   Martin Luther King, Jr. James M. Washington, ed. *A Testament of Hope* (New York, Harper San Francisco, 1986), 41.

86   *A Testament of Hope*, 221—222.

87   Simon Blackburn, ed. *The Oxford Dictionary of Philosophy* (New York, Oxford University Press, 1996), 169.

88 Hanes Walton. *The Political Philosophy of Dr. Martin Luther King, Jr.* (West Port, Conn. Greenwood Publications, 1971), 57—58.

89 Lawrence Kohlberg. *The Kohlberg Legacy for Helping Professions* (Birmingham, Alabama, R.E.P. Books, 1991), 159.

90 Michael J. Gorman. *Cruciformity: Paul's Narrative Spirituality of the Cross* (Grand Rapids/Cambridge, Wm. B. Eerdmans Publishing Co. 2001), 366.

91 Martin Luther King, Jr. *Strength to Love,* (Philadelphia, fortress Press, 1963), 23.

92 Taylor Branch. *Parting the Waters: America in the King Years 1954—63* (Touchstone Books, Simon & Schuster, 1988), 243.

93 Peter J. Ling. *Martin Luther King, Jr.* (New York, NY: Routledge, 2002), 60.

94 Martin Luther King, Jr. Clayborne Carson, ed. *The Autobiography of Martin Luther King, Jr.* (New York, NY: Time Warner Book Group, 1998), 118.

95 David J. Garrow. *Bearing the Cross: Martin Luther King Jr., and the Southern Christian Leadership Conference* (New York, NY: HarperCollins, 1986), 110.

96 David J. Garrow. *Bearing the Cross*, 110.

Chapter Six:
Martin Luther King Jr. and the Global Age:
Implications for International Peace and Social Justice

97 John R. Tyson, ed., *Invitation to Christian Spirituality: An Ecumenical Anthology* (New York, Oxford University Press, 1999), 459.

98   Taylor Branch. *Parting the Waters: America in the King Years 1954—63* (New York, Touch Stone by Published by Simon & Schuster, 1988), 214.

99   Carson Clayborne, ed. *The Autobiography of Martin Luther King, Jr.* (New York, Time Warner Books, 1988), 111.

100 Carson Clayborne, ed. The autobiography of Martin Luther King, Jr., 112.

101 David J. Garrow. *Bearing the Cross: Martin Luther King, Jr. and the Southern Christian Leadership Conference* (New York, HarperCollins Publishers, 1986), 91.

102. Martin Luther King, Jr. statement: "Call For an international Boycott of apartheid south Africa", human Rights Day, December 10, 1965. Public speech made at Hunter College, New York City, on human Rights Day. Reprinted by: southern Christian leaders Conference, 1983.

103 Basil Moore, editor, *The Challenge of Black Theology in South Africa* (Atlanta, Georgia, John Knox Press, 1974), viii. [Editors preface].

104 Edwin M. Yamauchi, *Africa and the Bible* (Grand Rapids, Michigan, Baker academic, 2004), 30.

105 Anthony T. Evans, *Are Blacks Spiritually Inferior to Whites? The Dispelling* of an American Myth (Wenonah, NJ: Renaissance Productions, Inc., 1992), 19.

106 Ibid., 15—16.

107 Ibid., 17.

108 Martin Luther King, Jr., Coretta Scott King, editor. *The Words of Martin Luther King, Jr.* (New York, Newmarker Press, 1967), 15.

109 Martin Luther King, Jr. statement: "Call For an international Boycott of apartheid South Africa", human Rights Day, December 10, 1965. Public speech made at Hunter College,

New York City, on human Rights Day. Reprinted by: Southern Christian Leaders Conference, 1983.

[110] Martin Luther King, Jr., Coretta Scott King, editor. *The Words of Martin Luther King,* Jr. (New York, Newmark Press, 1967), 19.

[111] Ibid. Hunter College speech, December, 10, 1965.

[112] Taylor Branch, *Pillar of Fire: America in the King Years 1963—65* (New York, NY: Simon 7 Schuster, 1998), 21.

[113] Ibid., 22.

[114] Ibid., 24.

[115] Taylor Branch, *Parting the Waters: America in the King Years 1954—63* (New York, NY: Simon & Schuster, 1988), 670.

[116] Harold M. Schulweis, "Two Prophets, one soul: Rev. Martin Luther King, Jr. and Rabbi Abraham Joshua Heschel,"9—8—2001http://www. theshalomcenter.org/node/122 (7 May, 2011).

[117] Martin Luther King, Jr. statement: "Call For an international Boycott of apartheid South Africa", Human Rights Day, December 10, 1965. Public speech made at Hunter College, New York City, on Human Rights Day. Reprinted by: Southern Christian Leaders Conference, 1983.

[118] Ibid.

[119] Coretta Scott King, ed. *The Martin Luther King, Jr. Companion* (New York, St. Martin's Press, 1993), 67.

[120] Martin Luther King, Jr., *Strength to Love* (Philadelphia, Fortress Press, 1981), 35.

[121] American Friends Services Committee, "Quakers will sponsor Trip of Montgomery leader to India. Press release: 26 January 1959. Special Collections at Boston University.

[122] Martin Luther King, Jr. and James Washington ed. *A Testament of Hope: The Essential Writings and Speeches*

of Martin Luther King, Jr. (New York, NY: Harper San Francisco, 1986), 24—25.

123 Staff Reporter, Atlanta—"Dr. King calls off Russian Trip." *Los Angeles Tribune*, 6 February 1956. [Newspaper article in Special Collections at Boston University].

124 Taylor Branch, *At Cannan's Edge: America in the king Years 1965—68* ((New York/London, Simon & Schuster, 2006), 556—7.

125 Ibid, 557.

126 Taylor Branch, *At Cannan's Edge, 620.*

127 Carson Clayborne, ed. *The Autobiography of Martin Luther King, Jr.*, 262.

128 Thomas Friedman. *The Lexus and the Olive Tree* (New York, Anchor Books, 2000), 9.

129 Martin Luther King, Jr. and James Washington ed. *A Testament of Hope: The Essential Writings and Speeches of Martin Luther King, Jr.* (New York, NY: HarperSanFrancisco, 1986), 254.

130 *A Testament of Hope, 617.*

131 U.S. Department of Health and Human Services Administration for Children and Families "About Human Trafficking" http://www.acf.hhs. gov/trafficking/about/index.html (18 June 2010).

132 U.S. Department of Health and Human Services Administration for Children and Families "Fact sheet: Human Trafficking," http://www. acf.hhs.gov/trafficking/about/fact_human.html (18 June 2010).

133 Martin Luther King, Jr. *The Measure of a Man* (Minneapolis, MN: Fortress Press, 1988), 43.

134 Anthony Kuhn, "Martin Luther King's story Plays on Beijing stage," *NPR June23. 2007,* http://www.npr.org/

templates/story/story._php?storyid=11330396 (16 June, 2010).

Chapter Seven:
I know I've been changed: Reconciliation and Social Reform

[135] John R. Tyson, ed., *Invitation to Christian Spirituality: An Ecumenical Anthology* (New York, Oxford University Press, 1999) 373.

[136] Robert Scofield, 'King's God: The unknown Faith of Dr. Martin Luther King, Jr. Tikkun Magazine 2009 http://www.tikkun.org/article.php/ nov_dec_09_scofield.html (1 August, 2010).

[137] Clayborne Carson, ed., *The Autobiography of Martin Luther King, Jr.* (New York, Time Warner Books, 1998), 56.

[138] Ibid.viii

[139] 117 Martin Luther King, Jr. *Strength to Love* (Philadelphia, Fortress Press, 1963), 105.

[140] Martin Luther King, Jr., *Why We Can't Wait* (New York, Signet Books, 1963), 81.

[141] Edmund Burke, Thoughts on the cause of the present discontents, 1770. In The Works of the Right Honorable Edmund Burke, edited by henry Froude, Oxford University Press, 1909, Volume 2, page 83, lines 7 to 16.

[142] Martin Luther King, Jr. & James M. Washington, ed., a Testament of hope: The essential Writings and speeches of Martin Luther King, Jr. (New York, HarperSanFrancisco, 1986), 217.

Chapter Eight:
New Leadership, Same Vision, New Voice

[143] John hope Franklin & Alfred a Moss, Jr., editors, *From Slavery to Freedom: A History of Negro Americans Sixth Edition* (New York, McGraw-Hill Publishing 1988), 246.

[144] Ibid., 34.

[145] Ibid., 80—81.

[146] Ibid., 33.

[147] John hope Franklin and Alfred A. Moss, Jr., *From Slavery to Freedom: A History of Negro Americans* (New York, McGraw-Hill, Inc., 1988), 244—245.

[148] Ibid., 247.

[149] Ibid., 247.

[150] Ibid., 247—8.

[151] Martin Luther King, Jr., *The Martin Luther King Jr. Companion: Quotations from the Speeches, Essays and Books of Martin Luther King, Jr.* (New York, St. Martin Press, 1993), 69. [Selected quote taken from the Why We Can't Wait book].

[152] Martin Luther King, Jr. & James M. Washington, ed., a *Testament of hope: The essential Writings and speeches of Martin Luther King, Jr.* (New York, Harper San Francisco, 1986), 621. [Selected quote taken from King's Where Do We Go From here? Book].

[153] Ibid., 249.

[154] John hope Franklin and Alfred A. Moss, Jr., *From Slavery to Freedom: A History of Negro Americans* (New York, McGraw-Hill, Inc., 1988), 248.

[155] King, *Why We Can't Wait*, 33.

[156] Henry Louis Gates, Jr. & Cornel West, *The Future of the Race* (New York, Vintage Books, 1996), 33.

157 Ibid., 58.

158 Henry Louis Gates, Jr. & Cornel West, *The Future of the Race* (New York, Vintage Books, 1996), 162.

159 bell hooks, *Where We Stand: Class Matters* (New York, NY: Routledge, 2000), 91.

160 *The Future of Race*, 168—9.

161 Ibid., 111.

162 Martin Luther King, Jr. & James M. Washington, ed., *A Testament of Hope*, 265. [selected quote from the Drum Major instinct sermon).

163 bell hooks, Where We stand, 94.

164 Ibid., 95.

165 John Hope Franklin and Alfred A. Moss, Jr., *From Slavery to Freedom: A History of Negro Americans* (New York, McGraw-Hill, Inc., 1988), 320.

166 Ibid., 320.

167 Ibid., 320.

168 Ibid., 322.

169 Timothy E. Fulop & Albert J. Raboteau editors. *African American Religion: Interpretive Essays in History and culture* (New York, NY: Routledge, 1997), 284—5.

170 Martin Luther King, Jr. *Why Can't We Wait*, 33.

171 Ibid.34—35.

172 Mark a. *Noll, God and Race in American Politics* (Prince and Oxford, Princeton University Press, 2008), 107.

173 Ibid., 35.

174 Martin Luther King, Jr. *The Measure of a Man* (Minneapolis, Fortress Press, 1988), 10—11.

175 Shelby Steele. *A Bound Man: Why We Are Excited About Obama and Why He Can't Win* (New York, Free Press, 2008), 7—8.

176 America.gov—Engaging the World. Minority Groups now one-Third of U. S. Population. http://www.america.gov/ st/washfile-english/2006/ July/20060707160631jmnamde irf0.2887079.html (2 June, 2009)

177 Ruth Morris, Gregory Lewis and Alva James-Johnson, "How We're Changing: For first time, nation's minority population tops 100 million," *South Florida Sun-Sentinel,* 17 May 2007, 1a (cover page).

178 Lewis V. Baldwin, *There is a Balm in Gilead: The Cultural Roots of Martin Luther King, Jr.* (Minneapolis, Fortress Press, 1991), 290.

179 David L. Lewis, *King A Biography* (Chicago, University of Illinois Press, 1978), 394.

Chapter Nine:
By This shall We Be Known: Where do we go from here?

180. Martin Luther King, Jr. Coretta Scott King, ed. *The Martin Luther King, Jr. Companion: Quotations from the Speeches, Essays and Books of Martin Luther King, Jr.* (New York, St. Martin Press, 1993), 101.

181 David J. Garrow, *Bearing the Cross: Martin Luther King, Jr., and the Southern Christian Leadership Conference* (New York, Perennial an imprint of HarperCollins Publishers, 1986), 533.

182 Martin Luther King, Jr. *Strength to Love* (Philadelphia, Fortress Press, 1963), 152.

183 Anthony Gross, ed., The Wit and Wisdom of Abraham Lincoln (New York, Barnes & noble Publishing, 1994), 226—227.

[184] Ibid. 227.

[185] Beth Nissen, "Cities jammed in worldwide protest of war in Iraq," *CNN. Com. U.S. 2003*, http://www.cnn.com/2003/us/02/15/sprj.irq.protests. main/ (8 June, 2010).

[186] Dan Carnevale, "Universities urged to Protect academic Freedom in the face of War," *The Chronicle of Higher Education 2003*, http://chronicle. com/article/universities-urged-to-Protect/14884/ (8 June, 2010).

[187] David J. Garrow, Bearing the *Cross: Martin Luther King, Jr., and the Southern Christian Leadership Conference* (Perennial/HarperCollins Publishers, 1986), 560

[188] Martin Luther King, Jr. James Washington, ed., *A Testament of Hope: The Essential Writings and Speeches of Martin Luther King, Jr.* (New York, Harper San Francisco, 1986), 240.

[189] Richard Lischer, The end of Words: *The Language of Reconciliation in a culture of Violence* (Grand Rapids/Cambridge, WM.B. Eerdmans, 2005), 16.

[190] Martin Luther King, Jr., *Strength to Love* (Philadelphia, Fortress Press, 1981), 151. Taken from King's sermon titled Pilgrimage to nonviolence.

[191] Martin Luther King, Jr. James Washington, ed., *A Testament of Hope* (New York, Harper San Francisco, 1986), 150. Kings speech to the Golden anniversary Conference of the urban league tilted, The Rising Tide of Racial Consciousness.

[192] Carter G. Woodson. *The Mis-Education of the Negro* (Trenton, NJ: African World Press, 1990), 26—27.

[193] Bill Maxwell, "I Had a Dream". *St. Petersburg Times*. 13 May, 2007. 1P.

[194] Bill Maxwell, "The once and Future Promise," *St. Petersburg Times*, 27 May 2007, 4.

[195] Carter G. Woodson. *The Mis-Education of the Negro*, 138.

196 Bill Maxwell, "I Had a Dream," Two years at Stillman: second in a three-part series. *St. Petersburg Times*, 13 May 2007, 5P.

197 Bill Maxwell, "a Dream lay Dying", *St. Petersburg Times*, 20 May, 2007, 5P.

198 Bill Maxwell, "a Dream lay Dying" St. Petersburg Times, (sources: U.S. news and World Report and staff reporting) 20 May, 2007, 5P.

199 Martin Luther King, Jr. ed. James Washington, Jr. *A Testament of Hope: The Essential Writings and Speeches of Martin Luther King, Jr.* (New York, Harper San Francisco, 1986), 150. (note the word negro is replaced with black in brackets to indicate current racial term used)

200 Bill Maxwell, a Dream lay Dying, "St. Petersburg Times, 20 May, 2007, 4P.

201 "A Dream Lay Dying, 4P.

202 Ibid., 4P

203 Ibid, 4P.

204 Maureen Downey, "new national dropout rates: 25 percent of all students: nearly 40 percent of black and Hispanic kids fail to graduate on time,"The Atlanta Journal-Constitution 2011, http://blogs.ajc.com/getschooled-blog/2010/06/02/new-national-dropout-rates-25-percent.html1 (27 February 2011).

205 Martin Luther King, Jr., James M. Washington, ed., *A Testament of Hope* (New York, Harper San Francisco, 1986), 139.

206 David J. Garrow, *Bearing the Cross* (New York: Perennial/Harper Collins Publishing, 1986), 181.

207 Mary Frances Berry, *And Justice for all: the United States Commission on Civil Rights and the Continuing struggle for freedom in America* (new york/Canada, Knopf, Borsoi Books, 2009),153.

208 Nick Kotz, *Judgment days: Lyndon Baines Johnson, Martin Luther King, Jr.,* (New York, First Mariner Books edition, 2005), 358.

209 Mary Frances Berry *And Justice for all: the United States Commission on Civil Rights and the Continuing struggle for Freedom in America,* 146.

210 *Bearing the Cross,* 581.

211 Martin Luther King, Jr. James M. Washington, ed. a Testament of hope (New York, Harper San Francisco, 1986), 106

212 *A Testament of Hope,* 274.t

213 Howard Thurman, *Jesus and the Disinherited* (Boston, Beacon Press, 1976), 17.

214 Ruby K. Payne, a *Framework for Understanding Poverty* (Highland, TX: aha! Process, Inc., 2005), 2.

215 *A Testament of Hope,* 614. (The bracket indicates the change from the term Negro to the more contemporary term black).

216 Ruby K. Payne, a *Framework for Understanding Poverty,* 6.

217 Ibid., 8.

218 Ibid., 8.

219 Ibid., 5.

220 Center for American Progress Task Force on Poverty, "From *Poverty to Prosperity: A National Strategy to Cut Poverty in Half,*" (11 June, 2010).

221 Heather Boushey, *"Unemployed—and Staying That Way,"* Center for American Progress, 2009, http://www. americanprogress.org/ issues/2009/05/employment.html (25 April, 2009).

222 Center for American Progress Task Force on Poverty, "From *Poverty to Prosperity: A National Strategy to Cut Poverty in*

Half," http://www.americanprogress.org/ issues/2007/04/ poverty_report.html (11 June, 2010).

223 *A Testament of Hope,* 558

224 Center for American Progress Task Force on Poverty, *"From Poverty to Prosperity: A National Strategy to Cut Poverty in Half,"* http://www. americanprogress.org/issues/2007/04/ poverty_report.html (11 June, 2010).

225 Center for American Progress Task Force on Poverty, *"From Poverty to Prosperity: A National Strategy to Cut Poverty in Half,"* http://www. americanprogress.org/issues/2007/04/ poverty_report.html (11 June, 2010).

226 David J. Garrow, *Bearing the Cross,* 582.

227 Ibid. 582.

Chapter Ten: Closing Reflections:
Martin Luther King Jr.'s Vision, Voice and Message Live

228 John Bunyan, *The Pilgrim's Progress* (Springdale, Pa: Whitaker house, 1973), 372—73.

229 Andrew M. Manis, *A Fire You Can't Put Out: The Civil Rights Life of Birmingham's Reverend Fred Shuttlesworth* (Tuscaloosa, Alabama, The University of Alabama Press, 1999), 435

230 Clayborne Carson, ed., *The Autobiography of Martin Luther King, Jr.* (New York, Time Warner Books, 1998), 173.

231 Andrew M. Manis, *A Fire You Can't Put Out* (Tuscaloosa, Alabama, The University of Alabama Press, 1999), 379.

232 T. S. Elliot, *Christianity and Culture: The Idea of a Christian Society and Notes towards the Definition of Culture* (New York/London, a harvest/ HBJ Book, 1977), 74.

233 Lewis Baldwin. *There is a Balm in Gilead: The Cultural Roots of Dr. Martin Luther King, Jr.* (Fortress Press, MN: 1992):161.

[234] Richard Lisher. *The Preacher King: Martin Luther King, Jr. And the Word That Moved America* (Oxford University Press, New York): 1995.

[235] Michael Eric Dyson. *I May Not Get There With You* (Free Press, New York, 2000):120.

[236] David Garrow, *Bearing the Cross,* 731.

[237] Martin Luther King, Jr., James M, Washington, ed., *A Testament of Hope* (New York, Harper San Francisco, 1986), 632.

INDEX

AUTHOR INDEX

BIBLIOGRAPHY

---- ✳ ----

Baldwin, Lewis. *There is a Balm in Gilead: The Cultural Roots of Dr. Martin Luther King, Jr.* Minneapolis, MN: Fortress Press, 1991. To *Make the Wounded Whole: The Cultural Legacy of Martin Luther King, Jr.* MN. Fortress Press.1991 *The Legacy of Martin Luther King, Jr. The Boundaries of Law, Politics, and Religion.* Indiana, university of Notre Dame Press, 2002.

Berry, Mary Frances. *And Justice for all: the United States Commission on Civil Rights and the Continuing Struggle for Freedom in America.* New York, Knopf Borzoi Books, 2009.

Branch, Taylor. *Parting the Waters: America in the King Years 1954-1963.* New York, Touchstone 1988. *Pillar of Fire: America in the King Years 1963—65.* New York, Simon and Schuster. 1998. *At Canaan's Edge: America in the King Years 1965—68.* New York, Simon and Schuster, 2006.

Burrow, Rufus, Jr. *God and Human Dignity: The Personalism, Theology, and Ethics of Martin Luther King, Jr.* Notre Dame Indiana, University Notre Dame Press, 2006.

Clayborne Carson ed. *The Autobiography of Martin Luther King, Jr.* New York, Warner Books, 1998.

Cone, James h. For *My People: Black Theology the Black Church?* Mary Knoll, New York, Orbis Books, 1984. *Martin and Malcolm and America: A Dream or a Nightmare.* Maryknoll, NY. Orbis Books, 1991

Coogan Michael D., ed. The new oxford annotated Bible: new Revised Standard Version with the apocrypha. New York, Oxford University Press, 2001.

Davies, Alfred T., ed. *The Pulpit Speaks on Race.* New York, Abingdon Press, 1965.

Drummond Lewis a. *The Evangelist.* Nashville, Tennessee, Word Publishing, 2001.

Dyson, Michael Eric. *April 4, 1968: Martin Luther King, Jr.'s Death and How it Changed America* (New York, Basic Civitas Books, 2008.

Elliot, T.S. *Christianity and Culture: The Century Edition 1888—1988.* New York, harvest/HBJ Book, 1977.

Evans, Anthony T. *Are Blacks Spiritually Inferior to Whites? The Dispelling of an American Myth.* Wenonah, NJ: Renaissance Productions, Inc., 1992.

Franklin, hope, John and Moss, Alfred a, Jr. *From Slavery to Freedom: A History of Negro Americans Sixth Edition.* New York, McGraw-Hill Publishing, 1988.

Garrow David, J. *Bearing the Cross: Martin Luther King, Jr., and the Southern Christian Leadership Conference.* New York, Harper Collins, 1986.

Gates, Henry Louis Jr., and Cornel West. *The Future of the Race.* New York, Vintage

Green, R.P.H. ed. *Saint Augustine, On Christian Doctrine.* New York, Oxford University Press, 1997.

Gorman, Michael J. *Cruicformity: Paul's Narrative Spirituality of the Cross.* Grand Rapids/Cambridge, Wm. B. Eerdmans Publishing Company, 2001.

Hauerwas, Stanley. *The Peaceable Kingdom*. Notre Dame Indiana, University of Notre Dame Press, 1983.

Hooks, Bell. *Where We Stand: Class Matters*. New York, Routledge, 2000.

Jenkins, Willis and McBride, Jennifer, ed. *Bonhoeffer and King: There Legacies and Import for Christian Social Thought*. Minneapolis, Fortress Press, 2010.

King, Martin Luther Jr., James M. Washington, ed. *Testament of Hope: The Essential Writings and Speeches of Martin Luther King, Jr.* San Francisco, Harper Collins, 1991. *The Measure of a Man*. Minneapolis, Fortress Press, 2001. *Stride Toward Freedom*. NY: Harper & Row, 1958. *Where Do We Go From Here: Chaos or Community?* New York, Harper & Row Publishers, 1967. *Why We Can't Wait*. NY: Penguin Books USA, 1963. *The Trumpet of Conscience*. New York, Harper & Row Publishers, 1967. Coretta Scott King, ed. The Martin Luther King, Jr., Companion: Quotations from the speeches, essays and Books of Martin Luther King, Jr. New York, St. Martin Press, 1993.

LaRue, Cleophus, J. ed. *Power in the Pulpit: How America's Most Effective Black Preachers Prepare Their Sermons* Louisville, Kentucky, Westminster John Knox Press, 202.

Lawson Steven and Payne Charles. *Debating the Civil Rights Movement, 1945—1968*. NY: Rowman Littlefield Publishers, 1998.

Kotz, nick. *Judgment Days: Lyndon Baines Johnson, Martin Luther King*, Jr. New York, First Mariner Books edition, 2005.

Lewis, David L. ed. *King a Biography Second Edition*. Chicago, University of Illinois Press, 1976.

Lischer, Richard. *The Preacher King:* New York: Oxford University Press 1995. *The End of Words: The Language of Reconciliation in a Culture of Violence*. Grand Rapids, Michigan, William B. Eerdmans Publishing Company, 2005.

Manis, Andrew, M. *A Fire You Can't Put Out: The Civil Rights Life of Birmingham's Reverend Fred Shuttlesworth.* Tuscaloosa, Alabama, The University of Alabama Press, 1999.

Marsh, Charles. *The Beloved Community: How Faith Shapes Social Justice from the Civil Rights Movement to Today.* New York, Perseus Book Group, 2005.

Moore, Basil, ed. *The Challenge of Black Theology in South Africa.* Atlanta, Georgia, John Knox Press, 1973.

Noll, Mark A. *God and Race in American Politics.* Princeton, NJ. Princeton University Press, 2008.

Payne, Ruby K. *A Framework for Understanding Poverty.* Highland, TX: aha! Process, Inc., 2005.

Proctor, Samuel DeWitt. *The Substance of Things Hoped For: A Memoir of African-American Faith.* Valley Forge, Pa: Judson Press, 1995.

Paris, Peter J. *The Social Teaching of the Black Churches.* Philadelphia: Fortress Press, 1985.

Steele, Shelby. *A Bound Man: Why We Are Excited About Obama and Why He Can't Win.* New York, Free Press, 2008.

Strain, Christopher B. *Pure Fire: Self-Defense as Activism in the Civil Rights Era.* Athens Georgia Press, 2005.

Thurman, Howard. *Jesus and the Disinherited.* Boston. Beacon Press, 1976.

Tyson, John R., ed. *Invitation to Christian Spirituality: An Ecumenical Anthology.* New Y, Oxford University Press, 1999.

Walton, Hanes. *The Political Philosophy of Dr. Martin Luther King, Jr.* West Port Conn. Greenwood Publications, 1971.

Wright, N. T. simply Christian. New York, Harper Collins Books, 2006.

Yamauchi, Edwin M. *Africa and the Bible.* Grand Rapids, Mi. Baker academic, 2004.

CPSIA information can be obtained
at www.ICGtesting.com
Printed in the USA
FFHW01n1504151018
48764060-52895FF